Living
BEYOND
Organic

nutritional
knowledge
redefined!

CHRISTINA AVANESS

TIARA PUBLISHING
Las Vegas, NV

nutritional
knowledge
redefined!

ISBN: 978-0-9815892-0-6

These statements have not been evaluated by the Food and Drug Administration. This publication contains the opinions and ideas of its author. It is intended to provide helpful information on a healthy lifestyle by means of cleansing and restorative foods and herbs. It is offered with the understanding that the author and the publisher are not rendering medical, health, or any other kind of clinical treatment advice in this book. The reader should consult a medical, health, or other competent professional before adopting any of the suggestions in this book or drawing inferences from it. This information is not intended to diagnose, treat, cure, or prevent any disease. Anyone with a medical condition should consult a physician. The author and publisher specifically disclaim all responsibility for any liability, loss, or risk, personal or otherwise, which is incurred as a consequence, directly or indirectly, of the use and application of any of the contents of this book.

Published by:

TIARA PUBLISHING
141 Torchwood Lane
Las Vegas, NV 89144
702.400.4161 or ara@LBOrganic.com

Cover and interior design by TLC Graphics, www.TLCGraphics.com
Cover: Tamara Dever; Interior: Erin Stark

Printed in Canada

Dedication

With love and appreciation, I dedicate this book
to my husband, Ara, who has been a pillar of strength,
always encouraging me to live up to my potential;
to my daughter Christara, who researched and contributed
to this endeavor; to my daughter Tiara for creating
the Kids Korner; to my mom for praying for me;
and to all my friends and family who have
embraced the Living Beyond Organic lifestyle.
I am honored to be a part of sharing the healing power
of Super Enzyme Foods.

Table of Contents

living beyond organic

Acknowledgments

ON BEHALF OF ALL THOSE WHO HAVE BEEN BLESSED WITH THE KNOWL-edge of Super Enzyme Foods, I wish to acknowledge the memory of Jonathan: Thunder: Wolf, Raphaology practitioner. We thank you for your passion and commitment to research, teaching, and healing and for guiding us through our healing process.

Sometimes we meet a rare individual who brings light into our life. Morning: Spirit: Wolf, professor of Raphaology, is one of those rare individuals. She is an extraordinary teacher and healer. She expanded my knowledge of the importance of food and sunlight, and their healing effects on the body.

For the past five years, she has been a fearless guide on our quest for health. Morning and Jonathan devoted a combined 35 years to compile their findings on foods and herbs and their healing properties through light frequency. Thanks to this life-saving information and its application, my husband, Ara, reversed heart disease and is here with us today, healthy and enjoying and appreciating life more than ever. When I thanked Morning for saving my husband's life, she said, "I gave you the information; you did the rest. And I love what you do with new information." Her words have inspired me to share this information with the world.

I also acknowledge the 50 years of research on enzymes by the late Dr. Edward Howell, author of *Enzyme Nutrition* and *Food Enzymes for Health & Longevity*, who in his nineties was still passionate about the research and breakthroughs yet to come, Jordan S. Rubin, N.M.D., and Joseph Brasco, M.D., for their work *Restoring Your Digestive Health.*

Contemporary expert on enzymes Hiromi Shinya, M.D., shares a professional and personal perspective in his work *The Enzyme*

Factor; this is a must-read. And finally, I wish to acknowledge those who invested countless hours of their time, energy, and expertise bringing this book to fruition, especially Antoinette Kuritz.

living beyond organic

Foreword

WHEN I MET CHRISTINA AVANESS, SHE WAS THE CONCERNED WIFE OF a man who had suffered a recent heart attack and was struggling with severe health problems. During their session with me, Tina and Ara learned that the body is capable of repairing damage to organs, muscles, and tissues by using herbs and changing internal conditions with food. They both took to heart these findings and the strong suggestion that they change their lifestyle by eating, drinking, relaxing, balancing, and alkalizing. I provided the herbs and the information, but it was up to them to make the lifestyle changes that true healing requires.

With the support of their two daughters, they immediately went home to make drastic, life-saving alterations. Never in my practice had I witnessed an entire family come together in support of each other with such rapid and caring action. Tina immediately cleared out and restocked every cupboard, closet, drawer, medicine cabinet, pantry, and refrigerator in their house with new stock and ingredients from the Super Enzyme Foods list. Inspired by the superlative taste of high enzyme foods and herbs and her husband's rapidly recovering health, she revitalized her tired cooking regimen.

Many conversations, phone calls, and informational exchanges took place between us over the ensuing months as Tina strived to make everything in her home healthful. She replaced beef with bison (buffalo), apples with pears, chicken with salmon, and iceberg lettuce with butter lettuce. Even though her family loved to eat chicken, they noticed that as their bodies detoxified from old, rancid fats, their new sense of taste and smell made chicken a sickening experience. Fast food that used to appeal to them no longer held any pleasure. They recognized the smell of rancid oils and synthetic chemicals coming from their old favorite restaurants. Their energy levels increased, skin cleared up, allergies disappeared, and pain and inflexibility diminished.

Tina marveled that what she used to think of as "healthier choices" such as apples, oranges, canola oil, turkey, and margarine were really substandard suggestions from commercial enterprises that had more to do with product placement than with health. Tina and her family have excitedly attended many classes offered in Raphaology Medicine and learned about the importance of reading and understanding food product labels, the digestive system as the root of either health or disease, the enzymatic characteristics that render foods digestible or indigestible, the nutritive value of enzyme-rich foods, and the medicinal properties of the many herbs Tina now uses. I have been overwhelmed by Tina's ability to comprehend unconventional information and apply it to daily life.

Our families have had many occasions to spend time together relaxing and enjoying ourselves, an essential element of healing ignored by many people. A poignant example occurred one summer while we were swimming in Lake Mead. Before this, Tina had, like many other people, assumed that if a food was organic it was good for you. While we were bobbing in the gentle waves near a small beach, some indelicate, brown, sulfur-smelling particles floated by us. When Tina asked me if I knew what the flotsam and jetsam were, I replied, "They're organic."

She looked rather skeptically at me and repeated her inquiry. I replied, "They're organic; does it matter what 'they' are?"

Her shocked expression told me I had perhaps gone too far. I allowed the information to settle in. A myriad of emotions played on her face. Finally, her eyes lit up and she said, "You mean that just because something's organic doesn't mean it's healthy?" We have had many a laugh recounting that story.

Tina has developed and perfected the Super Enzyme Foods from the Peak Frequency Foods list presented to her in Raphaology classes, making her meals into artistic presentations accompanied by masterful tastes found only in gourmet kitchens. Due to the warm and enduring friendship that has formed between us,

I have been honored and privileged to enjoy many of Tina's wondrous dishes.

Motivated by the information about Super Enzyme Foods and the what, how, and why of nutrition, Tina found a passion for "peaking" new recipes from family favorites and creating new ones based on the needs and desires of each family member and friend. She practices her art of food preparation and cooking with flair and tireless effort, infusing her recipes with a dash of love. When she first heard me speak of love as the most powerful ingredient that could be added to any food, with its immeasurable ability to change dis-ease to ease, Tina rolled her eyes at the corniness of the sentiment. Now she actually strives to put love in every morsel. Her kitchen became the testing ground for new taste sensations for her delighted family and for anyone else who happened to drop in hoping for a bite of one of her prized dishes, which of course filled them with love.

As a beautiful woman on the outside and with inner compassion and grace, Tina truly stands alone in her field. When she asked me if I would ever take on an intern, I told her I would love for her to present the life-changing ideals she has learned and would be honored to have her represent them on a large scale. I call her the "Seven-Star Chef" because her meals consist of foods that stimulate, nourish, and balance all seven of the human body's fundamental energy and hormone centers. With great sensitivity, she has taken into consideration multicultural palates, broad spectrum health needs, and the absolute fulfillment of taste, presenting healing foods with style and panache.

I could not be prouder of Tina's accomplishment in writing this book and do not hesitate to endorse *Living Beyond Organic*, for not only will your palate be thoroughly contented, but your health will also benefit from the standard she sets. You may even find that implementing Tina's guidelines will produce an unwritten result, the ingredient of palatable love added to your table of life.

— *Morning: Spirit: Wolf*

KALE for HEALTHY
| MUSCLES and BONES |

$\mathcal{I}$ntroduction

"Let food be thy medicine and medicine be thy food."
—HIPPOCRATES

FIVE YEARS AGO I ALMOST LOST MY HUSBAND TO HEART DISEASE AND found that I was in poor health myself. Conquering these conditions inspired me to write this book.Good health requires a balance of good nutrition, sunlight, exercise, and fun to counteract the damaging effects of stress. Your lifestyle choices determine the quality of these four elements. I redefine conventional knowledge about nutrition. Even if you eat organic and maintain what is considered by most to be a good, balanced diet, there is so much more to attaining good health. You need to understand the role of enzymes in the function of our bodies and how what we consume is directly related to maximizing the use of those enzymes. You need to Live Beyond Organic.

Living Beyond Organic is nutritional knowledge redefined. Not only do I reveal what to eat, how best to prepare it, and why, but I also share the secrets to a healthy kitchen, good daily habits, and suggestions for a healthier lifestyle.

The foundation of good health and longevity is eating Super Enzyme Foods. *Living Beyond Organic* presents the food choices that can change your life. I'll show you how to prepare delicious, nutritious meals that help you to detoxify, alkalize, replenish enzymes, restore health, and rejuvenate your body.

I am a nutritional consultant and food alchemist. I have achieved amazing results by combining the knowledge of ancient healing through food and herbs with my ability to create delicious recipes. Because I want to share the secrets of my success with you and know how difficult it is to change our lifestyles, I am providing you with a *21-Day Beyond Organic Menu Plan* with recipes to take the guesswork out of putting together healthful meals.

I have devoted the past six years to learning about the life-infusing properties of Super Enzyme Foods. By putting to work my knowledge of enzymes in conjunction with phyto-nutrients (plant medicine), I provided my family with foods that enabled my husband's recovery from a heart attack and restored all of our health. My recipes satisfy the gourmet palate and show how filet mignon with Béarnaise sauce and chocolate mousse can be good for you.

I had always cooked what I thought were healthy foods and oversaw my family's nutrition with diligence and care. I had accepted the mass marketing information as truth, and what we were eating was slowly poisoning us.

My husband was on antibiotics regularly. Ara would often get strep throat infections and would be on prescription medications so strong that he had to sleep a lot. In fact, misinformation and years of living in ignorance about real nutrition nearly took my husband's life.

At the same time, I lived in perpetual fear of my acute allergy attacks, especially those related to my allergy to peanuts and pesticides. I always carried an emergency epinephrine injector because of the risk of anaphylactic shock. I took allergy medication and drank caffeinated soft drinks regularly to suppress my symptoms. I ate refined carbohydrates such as white rice, enriched flour, and fatty meats like beef and chicken that caused fat to accumulate in my liver cells. I also had a history of teratomas (cystic uterine growths), chronic fatigue, and severe premenstrual syndrome, which caused mood swings and irritability. Some mornings I would wake up with such crippling arthritic back pain that I couldn't get out of bed. I was not yet 40, and, ironically, considered myself healthy!

Our daughters visited the pediatrician often for colds, flu, fever, and coughs. They took acetaminophen and cough syrup with such regularity that they even had a favorite flavor. My older daughter, Christara, has always been a perfectionist and overachiever. In spite of eating chicken fingers and fries, pancakes with turkey sausages, waffles with bacon, and carrot sticks and apples with ranch dressing, she was underweight and lacked energy. My younger daughter, Tiara, had kidney problems due to dehydration at the tender age of 6. She had severe mood swings due to hormonal imbalance, and she suffered from nightmares due to poor digestion.

We ate out occasionally, but we were far from junk food consumers. I prided myself in serving home-cooked meals. By almost anyone's standards, we were eating well—or so I thought. Yet all of us were suffering from weak immunity perpetuated by an enzyme-depleted diet. Like everyone else, we were susceptible to seasonal colds and flu.

Then in 2002, Ara had a heart attack and also was diagnosed with poor kidney function, near liver failure, and clogged arteries due to high cholesterol. About the same time, I discovered I had fatty liver disease, which afflicts about a third of adults in the U.S. Much like superheroes fighting crime, our family joined forces to fight the disease that threatened my husband's life.

Making the seemingly irrational choice not to follow the advice of highly credentialed physicians who recommended that Ara take cholesterol and blood pressure drugs, we felt compelled to consider a friend's suggestion to meet his "Doc," a natural healer.

Meeting Doc was like meeting Mother Nature. She was very kind, and even though my husband's condition was critical, she never alarmed us. Nevertheless, I did have strong reservations about alternative natural healing. After all, until this point in my life I had been comfortable with modern medicine. Her method included an herbal program to repair damage and a food program to boost and maintain organ function. She made it clear that to effect positive change we needed to follow her instructions to the letter. She asked that we try her approach for three months before starting Ara on prescription medication.

Some of the changes we made in our eating habits seemed strange at first. Every morning Ara had one cup of fresh papaya to boost his kidney function and half a juiced lemon to activate the liver bile. To manage his high blood pressure, he took hawthorne berry herb as needed and to flush his kidneys, he drank a glass of spring water with a quarter-teaspoon of RealSalt. To lower his cholestrol (LDL), he ate half an avocado with two tablespoons of first cold-pressed (FCP) extra virgin olive oil, and to boost/repair his liver he had crookneck squash and Hawthorne leaf herb. Due to the critical nature of his disease, Ara also had natural ethylene diamine tetra-acetic acid (EDTA) chelation therapy—a chemical process that binds molecules so they can be removed from the body—administered by a physician. With this routine and a few other simple foods and herbs, his blood pressure and cholesterol levels stabilized.

Ara lowered his LDL (bad cholesterol) level, which had been off the charts, in a period of three months; fully recovered from the heart attack in one year; and stabilized his critically high blood pressure all without any prescription medication or surgery. Now he is in his mid-fifties; his LDL is below 100, and his blood pressure is 120/70 to 130/80. He can race with Christara, who was on her school's track team, and he has the stamina to hike with our 12-year-old Tiara.

I now have a healthy liver, naturally eliminated a teratoma, dissolved gallstones, no longer suffer from chronic allergies, and have more energy than ever. I was determined to be well, and through dedication to this lifestyle, combined with the following regimen, I was able to achieve results.

Eating crookneck squash regularly helped improve my liver function; drinking lemon juice and olive oil with a dash of Real-Salt helped cleanse my liver. Eating fresh alfalfa and wheat berry sprouts whenever possible and taking therapies of dandelion root tea periodically dissolved my gallstones. To boost my immune system I take B-complex vitamin (liquid from a food source with potassium), bee pollen, and Royal Jelly. These supplements and exposure to 20 minutes of morning sunlight (with olive oil applied topically for skin nutrition and protection) eliminated the need for allergy medications. A therapy using food grade hydrogen peroxide helped me to eliminate a teratoma. These remedies were combined with nutrition from Super Enzyme Foods and herbal extracts to repair damage.

Before childbearing, I exercised regularly and weighed 110 pounds. At the height of my toxicity and after my second child, I weighed 148 pounds. I am now in my mid-forties and even though I don't work out as vigorously as I used to, I am comfortable at 118 to 121 pounds. My friends and family have commented that my skin has a healthy glow and that I look younger than I did 10 years ago.

When Christara had her first session of Raphaology, based on the healing practices of ancient indigenous cultures, we found out she suffered from dehydration, malnutrition, an impacted colon, and a damaged spleen. Super Enzyme Foods and herbal remedies provided the tools to heal her body. Now her digestive system is restored and her spleen is fully functioning. Christara continues to be an A student, but she now takes time to relax and enjoy herself. She enjoys martial arts, swimming, and dancing and is majoring in biochemistry at the University of Southern California.

Tiara's kidneys are now fully functioning. She no longer suffers from nightmares. She has a reputation for being the "healthy girl" at school because she gladly shares nutritional information with her friends. Tiara enjoys singing, dancing, and sharing health tips in the Kids Korner of the *Living Beyond Organic* Web site.

So much of life is a matter of choice, but in this case the choice is an imperative. We are ticking time bombs. How do we stand a chance when processed foods, empty carbohydrates, and a plethora of refined and artificial sweeteners as well as genetically altered produce and meat products have become staples in our diets? We are threatened with serious illness. You can continue as you are, or you can take charge of your health by replacing the above-mentioned foods with nourishment that enhances your life force instead of depleting it. Eliminate these food imposters before they eliminate you. The decision to claim your health is yours. The fact that you are reading these words right now means that you are ready to receive this vital, precious, and life-saving information.

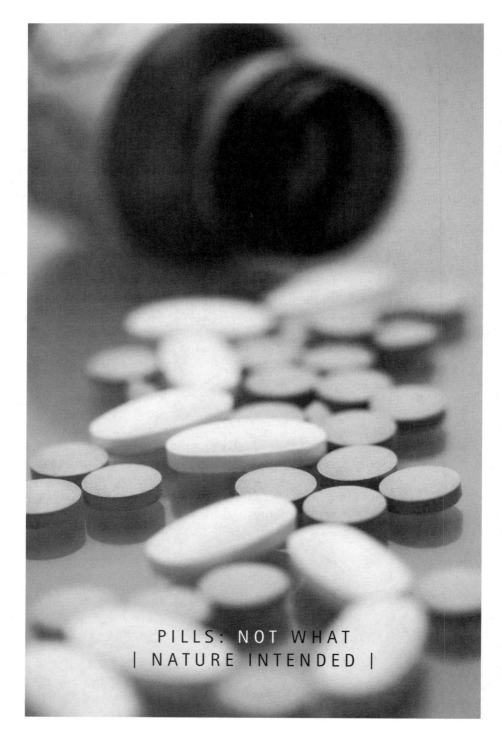

PILLS: NOT WHAT
| NATURE INTENDED |

Just because
it's organic
doesn't mean
it's good for you.

CHAPTER ONE

Today's Health Crisis

NEW DIETS SEEM TO HIT THE MARKET EVERY WEEK. BUT IF DIETS WORK, why are there so many? Why are so many Americans still overweight? Why are so many of us suffering from or on the verge of dis-ease? It's because diets don't work. Diets are temporary measures, typically focused on weight loss rather than on good health.

Approximately 25 percent of Americans are obese. Almost two-thirds are overweight. Heart disease, diabetes, and a host of other illnesses are on the rise. Dieting isn't enough. Eating the same old foods in smaller portions or eating prepackaged, overprocessed food may help you to lose weight. But it will not maximize your health.

We are constantly tempted by a barrage of TV ads for fast, frozen, enriched, sugar-laden food. We also are drowning in a sea of ads for medications. Can't sleep? Take a pill! Have digestive tract problems? Try one of the new yogurt cultures. Is acid reflux your problem? What about headaches, muscle pain, and joint aches? Suffer with allergies or asthma? Over-the-counter pills, liquids, and inhalers abound. If you listen carefully to the disclaimers, you'll hear in rapid-fire succession the possible side effects that ironically sometimes include the very symptom you are trying to alleviate. The medications being pushed on us are not cures. At best, they mitigate symptoms. But symptoms are the body's way of signaling us that something is amiss. Alleviating the symptoms only masks the underlying problem.

While genetic predisposition might be a contributing factor for some of the dis-ease we incur, much of it is the result of lifestyle choices, starting with the food that we eat. If you want to feel better and be healthier, you will have to reconsider what you eat.

Regardless of how much we exercise or how healthy we believe our diet to be, many of us suffer from hidden malnutrition due to an overworked digestive tract. If you regularly experience fatigue, acidity, allergies, constipation, or headaches, you actually are experiencing the symptoms of malnutrition related to poor digestive function due to consumption of dead, enzyme-depleted food.

At its best, food nourishes while creating balance; at anything less than its best, it depletes the body and creates toxicity. Our food choices are often based on what is familiar, what seems easiest, and what our families will eat. Implementing change can take time and planning. But to eat healthfully, we must educate ourselves and then act accordingly.

Let's take a look at heart disease, the number one cause of death in our country for the past 80 years. According to the CDC (Center for Disease Control), 654,092 people died of heart disease in the United States in 2004. And while men once were more likely to succumb to it, the opposite is now true: according to the National Center for Health Statistics, women represented 51 percent of U.S. heart-related deaths in 2001. Heart disease cost this country $260 billion in 2002, but this monetary figure is insignificant when weighed against the devastating loss of hundreds of thousands of human lives and the subsequent trauma to the surviving family members and loved ones.

I feel compelled to share my experience in *Living Beyond Organic* because I have learned that dis-ease is preventable. The most powerful healing tool is nutrition. Beginning by nourishing the body with half an avocado and two tablespoons of first cold-pressed extra virgin olive oil each day eliminates the toxic buildup that causes dis-ease. The annual expense will be about $300. That's the cost of about 20 pizzas. My husband is living proof that this works. After his heart attack, he began this regimen and cleared up excess fatty toxins. It is rare that he misses his daily intake of these essential fatty acids along with fresh papaya and lemon juice for his kidney function and liver respectively.

Additional evidence from the American Heart Association (AHA) says that those diagnosed with cardiovascular disease can benefit from a Mediterranean-style diet rich in fruits, vegetables, grains, fish, beans, and olive oil. And French researchers who monitored the death rates of 600 men and women who had had a heart attack found that 50 percent of those who followed a Mediterranean-style diet (but higher in omega-3 fatty acids than the AHA's Therapeutic Lifestyle Changes diet guidelines) had a 70 percent lower rate of recurring heart disease over the following 10 years.

Choosing to Live Beyond Organic is letting go of old information and habits that block you from a state of wellness and balance. We all want to be healthy. *Living Beyond Organic* promotes health. Give this new lifestyle a chance and prepare to feel better.

PAPAYA for AN
| ENZYME INFUSION |

*It's about being
balanced, and food
is only the beginning.*

C H A P T E R   T W O

What Is Living Beyond Organic?

In *Living Beyond Organic*, we tap into the healing power of food to replenish enzymes, to strengthen our immune systems, to restore our health, and to rejuvenate our bodies.

We live in a world of supply and demand. Due to the societal dependence on convenience, we have fast food and microwaves. We have instant breakfast, instant coffee, frozen dinners, dough-nuts, and genetically modified food with shelf lives longer than our life expectancy! The time has come to prevent dis-ease, not just treat its symptoms. And to do so, we must carefully consider what we consume.

Without food, we cannot survive. Food provides the energy we need to function. But how much thought do we typically give to which foods are the best energy sources? Most of us give more thought to weight gain and calories than to the nutritional value of our food.

"Organic" has become the buzzword for healthy food. If the word "organic" is on the label, we tend to trust that the con-tents are beneficial to our health and well-being. But there is more to being healthy. *Living Beyond Organic* is about under-standing the essential attributes of food and how they relate to optimum health.

Next time you shop for an organic product you should know that a product labeled "organic" must contain at least 95 percent organic ingredients.

But what about the remainder? Products labeled "100 percent organic" contain all organically produced ingredients excluding water and salt, which means they could contain tap water and iodized salt. So first we need to consider *what* we are eating, not whether the food is organic. For a more complete understanding of what organic means according to the National Organic Program that sets the standards, refer to: (*www.ams.usda.gov/nop/indexIE.htm*).

Just Because It Says "Organic" Doesn't Mean It's Good for You

Many companies put the word "organic" in bold bright letters on their products. They are counting on the media hype to convince you that their products are healthier. Just because it says "organic" on the label doesn't mean it's good for you.

It is what you are eating that is most important.

For example, the next time you look at the label of a carton of sour cream, you should see one ingredient: Grade A sour cream. Period. Surprisingly, you won't find many sour cream labels that say that. Most have other ingredients such as: cultured Grade A pasteurized organic light cream and organic nonfat milk, guar gum, carrageenan, locust bean gum, vitamin A palmitate. These ingredients appear on the labels from companies that make healthy products, but ingredients are often changed or substituted. You must learn what to look for and always check the label, even if you have used the product before.

Learning about Super Enzyme Foods and adapting our lifestyle brought my family to optimal health. For us this means that we are free of prescription medications, and except for check-ups we have not needed to see a medical doctor. With the knowledge of Super Enzyme Foods you and your family can do it too.

Living Beyond Organic is more than simply choosing to buy organic foods; it is knowing which foods and combinations of foods will lead to a higher level of health. If you are concerned that you can't afford organic food, rest assured that you will benefit from the information in this book as long as you are eating properly washed and prepared Super Enzyme Foods, organic or not. Fresh fruits and vegetables need to be washed thoroughly. I use one drop of food-grade hydrogen peroxide when I rinse my produce to eliminate possible contamination from pesticides and germs from handlers.

Ignorance Is Not Bliss

In fact, ignorance is death when it comes to nutrition. I know because we came close to it.

Before embracing this lifestyle, my family and I were going along with our usual routine. Like hamsters on a wheel, we were moving a mile a minute but getting nowhere fast, with one exception: our health was on the fast track to dis-ease.

We were literally clueless about nutrition and the vital role it plays in maintaining good health. As a wife and mother, I felt responsible to learn about nutrition and what I could do to provide my family with healthy meals, and I believed I had done so. Unfortunately, I was making choices based on misinformation. I was cooking at home during the week and eating out or ordering in on the weekends. Because I enjoy cooking, I took pride in preparing "gourmet meals" for my family. My family's favorites included oyster chicken with yaki-soba noodles, beef filet with Béarnaise sauce, real or imitation crabmeat, California rolls with white rice, grilled lemon chicken salad with white wine vinaigrette, and more.

When I wanted to take a break from the kitchen, we would go out for sushi and Chinese food such as chicken chow mein or shrimp fried rice, always avoiding the beef entrees because we believed chicken was "better for you." We even went on fruit-and-veggie-only days to "cleanse" so we felt better about having takeout pizza and gourmet burritos and chicken entrees that were regularly available in our home. We always felt guilty giving in to our taste buds.

We were operating on the misinformation that chicken was OK, that free range chicken was really healthful, and that eating beef occasionally was OK too, especially if it was organically grown or hormone free. Sound familiar? Well, I discovered that by

what is living beyond organic?

feeding my family this way, we were expeditiously and ignorantly headed toward serious illness.

For most of us, it takes a near-death experience to get us to pay attention to what we eat. You can learn from our experience. Don't wait to have a heart attack or develop diabetes, high blood pressure, or cancer to start being aware of what you eat and how to take care of your health.

I learned and applied a basic but effective concept: Give up something you think is good for something far better. If you feel stressed, tired, or bloated; if you are experiencing aches and pains; if you feel optimum health is eluding you; or if you feel you could be making better choices for yourself and your family, the information that follows is essential.

*If you believe that
enzymes don't survive
in the stomach, think again.*

CHAPTER THREE

Enzymes:
The Superheroes
of the Digestive System

*"Enzymes are the acting agents that cause the body to use
carbohydrates, vitamins, proteins, fats and minerals, which are
the complex foundation that support our lives. Enzymes are the life
force, vitamins and minerals are the tools, and proteins, fats,
and carbohydrates are the material that we are made of.
Sustain this foundation in balanced proportions and
we achieve and maintain vitality, health and passion."*

—JONATHAN: THUNDER: WOLF, D.R.M.

WHAT IS ENZYME POTENTIAL? ACCORDING TO DR. HOWELL, "WE inherit a certain enzyme potential at birth. Other things being equal you live as long as your body has enzyme activity factors to make enzymes from."

Enzymes are more than catalysts. Enzymes possess life energy and have dual capabilities, functioning both chemically and biologically. Enzymes are the super energy that makes all digestive processes and bodily functions possible.

Enzyme types. We depend on metabolic enzymes to keep our body functioning, digestive enzymes to digest our food, and exogenous enzymes derived from raw foods to start digestion.

Metabolic enzymes are essential to every aspect of life. They are powerful and dependable. They are so efficient we don't have to think about things such as breathing, sleeping, and thinking, digesting our food, building new muscle, or defending ourselves from harmful substances. Most important, they swiftly eliminate unwanted chemicals and waste material from the body.

Body and organ functions depend on the presence of enzymes. Hair growth, eyesight, attention span, cell renewal, cell repair, free-radical scavenging, alertness, circulation, and digestion—all rely on enzymatic activity.

Digestive enzymes unlock the benefits of nutrients. Four main categories of digestive enzymes rescue nutrients from our food and deliver them safely to nourish our body. **Amylase** serves to digest carbohydrates. **Protease** works to digest proteins. **Lipase** breaks down fats. **Lactase** assists in breaking down lactose. By accessing the nutrients stored inside food, enzymes serve to build, maintain, and protect the body.

The enzymes in raw foods are destroyed by overcooking. Exposure to a mere 118 degrees Fahrenheit for 30 minutes denatures enzymes. The enzyme-less food can no longer digest itself in the upper stomach. In the absence of active peristalsis and hydrochloric acid, this dead food is vulnerable to bacteria growth. Including raw foods at each meal and taking digestive enzyme supplements with cooked food are both helpful.

Highly processed foods are devoid of any enzymes. Dead foods which are depleted of enzymes by refinement, enrichment, and over-processing stress every part of the digestive system, creating acidity from overproduction of hydrochloric acid and causing malnutrition because these foods have no usable nutrients. The pancreas gradually is impaired and is no longer able to produce alkalizing enzymes, the only neutralizing force against the harmful, highly acidic conditions. Years of ingesting highly processed foods progressively increases the acidity level, destroys the ability to digest food and assimilate essential nutrients, and damages digestive organs.

Enzyme Sources

Enzymes come from two sources the food we eat and our own bodies. If we do not get an adequate supply of enzymes through what we eat, our bodies are taxed to produce them. The body can produce enzymes, but this capability is limited due to constant exposure to toxicity from the environment and improper nutrition. Eating low-enzyme or enzyme-depleted food strains the digestive organs because the body is forced to make additional enzymes to complete digestion. Since the pancreas has a limited enzyme production capability, consuming low-enzyme foods puts a hold on the body's other important metabolic functions like burning body fat, balancing blood sugar, breaking down protein, assimilating minerals, and so on. What makes Super Enzyme Foods superior is that they come to the digestion party with their own enzymes.

The average American subsists on dead food, food that is enzyme-depleted due to overcooking, over-processing, artificial preservatives, coloring, sweetening, and hydrogenation. It is only a matter of time before the Modern American Diet—or MAD—choices catch up with us.

When we consume enzyme-depleted food, we start a chain reaction:

- Indigestion
- Acidity, which breeds harmful bacteria
- Harmful bacteria, which weaken our immune system
- Weakened immunity, which makes us more susceptible to virus

All of the above, plus hormonal imbalance, poor circulation, and poor digestion lead to dis-ease, conditions which are directly related to what we eat. To avoid getting sick the human body needs Super Enzyme Foods (see list on page 38). Built-up toxicity in the body can cause or aggravate existing dis-ease conditions, so detoxifying is the imperative first step in reclaiming good health. As you detoxify, you will begin to experience results in three to six weeks. Stay on course and you will manifest change in your life. The reward is your health.

What You Need to Know
about the Digestive System

Now that you know that the basis of digestion is founded in enzymatic activity (not calorie content), you won't have to worry about counting calories from carbs, sugars, proteins, and fats ever again! However, do consider the digestive process in making your food choices.

- The process starts when we see a scrumptious meal, get a whiff of a delectable aroma, or even think about tasty food. The mouth produces saliva, and the stomach and small intestines are activated to produce digestive juices. The pancreas makes alkalizing enzymes and the liver begins to form bile.

- Chewing 15 to 30 times per bite makes the rest of the process a lot easier. In some cases, it can prevent indigestion symptoms by increasing the surface area of the food in preparation for the digestive enzymes in the stomach. Your saliva also contains amylase, an enzyme that helps to break down carbohydrates.

- After being chewed and swallowed, the food (at this stage referred to as a bolus) travels down the throat to the esophagus. Through rhythmic muscle movements (also known as peristalsis), the esophagus facilitates the movement of the bolus through the cardiac valve and into the upper/cardiac stomach where the enzymes break down the food for approximately 30 minutes.

- The food descends to the lower part of the stomach where hydrochloric acid, also referred to as gastric acid, will continue the digestive process. This strong acid tenderizes the food, kills bacteria, and activates the fat-and-protein-digesting enzymes. It is crucial to understand that the saliva digests the carbohydrates (starches) while the proteins and fats are activated by acids. Fresh, raw, enzyme-rich foods must be incorporated into every meal, or proper digestion cannot occur.

- The lower stomach has strong muscular walls that churn the bolus. The resulting soupy mixture of partially digested food and stomach acid is called chyme.

- The chyme travels through the pyloric valve to the first part of the small intestine, called the duodenum, to the final part of the small intestine, known as the ileum. Acidic bile, produced by the liver and stored in the gallbladder, is delivered to the duodenum and further dissolves the food.

- Meanwhile, alkalizing enzymes from the pancreas balance the pH in the small intestine by neutralizing the acidity in preparation for nutrient absorption. Other digestive enzymes help metabolize the food so that the nutrients are broken into individual vitamins, minerals, proteins, and so on, and can be taken via blood fluid exchange to the liver for purification. Foods that are difficult to digest require enormous amounts of digestive juices and will wait until enough is present.

- Meanwhile, these foods putrefy and release massive amounts of toxins. In an effort to store and neutralize the toxins, the liver begins to degenerate, fails to remove bacteria, grows sluggish, and produces sticky bile that can easily develop into gallstones. The abnormal bile cannot effectively digest and utilize fats, so the liver stores these toxic deposits in adipose tissue under the skin and in organs. This simple protective measure results in what we have come to recognize as obesity.

- The liquid remains of food flow into the colon through the ileocecal valve. Mineral deficiency causes this valve to remain slightly open, leaking a backwash of colon fluids into the small intestine where harmful yeast growth and bloating can result. The appendix releases good bacteria into the passing fluid, which separates fluid from fiber, allowing fiber to move along by assisting in fluid absorption and the transport of remaining nutrients through the colon walls.

- The liver cleans up pharmaceutical toxins, environmental contaminants, harmful alcohols, and synthetic food additives, discarding them through the colon. A dysfunctional liver will go into protection mode by creating excess enzymes, which in turn block or inhibit the liver's functions. This creates scar tissue and slimy, poor quality bile, which leads to poor digestion and the formation of stones.

- The fiber waste travels upward along the ascending colon, across the abdomen in the transverse colon, back down the other side of the body in the descending colon, and then out through the sigmoid colon. The rectum holds back the solid waste until it can be excreted.

When digestive acids are in the correct proportions through consumption of exogenous enzymes (from raw foods), we maintain a balanced pH level. Maintaining this balance is important because it helps boost our immune system. Subsequently, every other system in the body will perform better. When we consume processed, over-cooked, enzyme-depleted food, it increases our acidity level by adding stress on the digestive system to produce more hydrochloric acid. Thus, enzymes and accompanying vitamins, minerals, fats, and proteins are destroyed. These remnants accumulate in the form of stored toxins.

Digestive stress occurs when the pancreas is forced to work overtime trying to keep up with the production of alkalizing enzymes to neutralize excess acidity. When this process fails, acidity levels rise and bacteria thrive and attack our organs. Symptoms might include sharp pain, gas, or bloating. Our immunity weakens, and we become more susceptible to viruses that attack our tissues such as cold sores, sore throat, and body ache. If these conditions continue, the eventual result is fungus in the system. Symptoms include nail fungus, athlete's foot, and trembling, which in advanced stages lead to nerve damage.

A common symptom of digestive stress we are all familiar with is heartburn.

Heartburn occurs when hydrochloric acid backs up into the esophagus. Antacids are the modern-day approach, but one of the following natural recipes will just as effectively neutralize acidity without suppressing the immune system and adversely altering the biochemistry of the body. Any of these solutions work well for us at home:

- ¼ teaspoon RealSalt and half a juiced lemon in 8 ounces of spring water
- ¼ teaspoon organic baking soda and half a juiced lemon in 4 ounces of spring water

- 1 teaspoon red wine vinegar with a glass of water
- Raw red potato slices with a dash of RealSalt
- Chamomile/Peppermint Tea Infusion (*see recipe on page 155*)
- A glass of goat's milk

To avoid heartburn:
- Avoid dead food (over-processed, no enzyme).
- Consume more live food (raw, high enzyme).
- Drink plenty of pure water every day
  (aids digestion and flushes toxins).
- Avoid antacids containing aluminum.

"The aluminum in antacids is difficult to absorb. It remains in the intestines, where it can cause dryness and constipation. Aluminum has been implicated in Alzheimer's disease and may contribute to osteoporosis. Antacids are a classic example of a drug that masks the symptoms of a disease instead of treating its causes."
— JOSEPH BRASCO, M.D., GASTROENTEROLOGIST

Aluminum is lurking in many products that you may not suspect. These are just a few of the products to beware of:

- Antiperspirant
- Baking powder
- Commercial baked goods
- Self-rising flour
- Conventional cake mix
- Conventional pancake batter
- Ready-made pie crust
- Nondairy creamers
- Processed cheese
- Hemorrhoid medication
- Table salt
- Aluminum beverage cans
- Aluminum foil
- Anti-dandruff preparations
- Feminine douches

If you are lucky enough not to be using any of the products listed above, there is another source of potential toxins including aluminum we need to be aware of—our local water supply. Many cities add fluoride (a by-product of aluminum) to the water supply to promote strong teeth. More in the water section.

Cola and Conventional Soft Drinks

Colas shut down our body's ability to detoxify. I drank cola for many years to control my allergy symptoms, for an energy boost, and because it became a habit. Six years ago, I stopped drinking colas cold turkey and I feel better than ever!

Colas represent the largest amount of fluid consumed in the world today. It's no wonder that 75 percent of Americans suffer from chronic dehydration. Have you ever seen children order water in a restaurant? Chances are you haven't; instead, most kids order soda. That's because media hype and advertising targets them, and parents acquiesce to the status quo. I hope to shed some light on the subject. Parents need to know that colas cause:

- Dehydration, which slows metabolism and triggers loss of energy, constipation, and premature aging

- Avoidance of drinking water, which is the only fluid the body can use to conduct all metabolic processes

A mere 2 percent drop in body water can trigger fuzzy short-term memory, trouble with basic math, and difficulty focusing on the computer screen or printed page. Thirty percent of Americans today suffer from cola dis-ease. Its symptoms include:

- Bulging eyes
- Darkening of the whites of the eyes
- Hair loss
- Fatigue
- Weakened immunity
- Impaired bowel function
- Decreased hormone production
- Sexual dysfunction

Colas cause phosphoric acid bombardment. Wondering how your stomach is surviving it? Your body has amazing protective abilities. Under constant attack from highly acidic contamination, the body forms multiple layers of mucous plaque to encapsulate the toxins. This mucoid plaque can develop to the consistency of rubber, and although it serves as a protective mechanism, it is a bad condition that needs to be remedied. It is ironic that grade school children can do science projects on the negative effects of cola (corrodes teeth, dissolves raw meat, and shines pennies) and still drink it! The first step is to stop drinking colas.

Our body needs CLEAN WATER. Dehydration speeds up the AGING process.

Water, Water, Everywhere
Are You Drinking Enough?

The exact number of cells in the human body is unknown, but estimates range from 50 trillion to 100 trillion. Each individual cell is more complex in its function than a large metropolis. Our cells are primarily devoted to the tasks of taking in nutrients, discarding waste, and renewing themselves.

The body needs more than nutrients from food. Pure water is the only fluid that hydrates cells: drinking anything else like juices, tea, or soda pop, does not count. Living cells need the precious elixir we call water to sustain life.

You can survive without food but not without water.

We are made of approximately 75 percent water. The water content in the body is distributed in different compartments. For example, muscle tissue is about 75 percent water; blood contains about 83 percent water; body fat contains about 25 percent; and bone has 22 percent. We need lots of water to maintain a healthy body.

This means that we must replenish this precious resource adequately on a daily basis to prevent premature aging of the cells. We have 4.5 gallons of body fluid that need to be exchanged every nine days. We must consume a half gallon (64 ounces, or 8 eight-ounce glasses) of water each day to accomplish this. Otherwise, all lymph fluids, blood fluids, and cell fluids grow stagnant in the same way standing water stagnates.

The quality of the water we consume is of paramount importance. The best choice that is readily available and affordable is natural spring or artesian water. There are many choices on the market such as Arrowhead Mountain Spring, Crystal Geyser, Fiji, and others. Those listed above are readily available, affordable, and bottled at the source. We use Mountain Valley Spring Water because it is higher in alkalinity than most other brands (7.8 pH) and is bottled in glass.

It is important to know that because water is a living element, it maintains its life force by using sunlight, air, and constant movement. This is one of the reasons why natural spring water bottled at the source has an expiration date. Water absorbs pure light from the sun, just as plants do, so drinking water is a great way to take the full light spectrum into our body along with daily morning sunlight 20 to 30 minutes and, of course, lots of Super Enzyme Foods.

Once you choose a brand of water, store it in a glass or ceramic dispenser rather than plastic. It is a good idea to invest in a glass bottle for your water cooler. If the water is in plastic bottles and exposed to heat, it causes the plastic to release toxins which contaminate the water. Never reuse or refill plastic water bottles. They are a breeding ground for bacteria. It is best to avoid using individual plastic bottled water if possible. I encourage you to use a personal water bottle in stainless steel or glass that can be sanitized and reused. I use 1 drop of H_2O_2 (food-grade hydrogen peroxide) per gallon of water to:

- Neutralize possible contamination
- Oxygenate the water
- Increase water surface tension
- More readily hydrate cells

Do not mistake regular hydrogen peroxide found at the grocery store at a fraction of the cost for food-grade hydrogen peroxide. Food-grade hydrogen peroxide is perishable and must be refrigerated.

Warning: *Use caution when handling this substance. It may burn on contact with skin. If this occurs, rinse affected area under cold running water.*

Food-grade hydrogen peroxide must be diluted when taken internally. We are very careful when using it, as it can stimulate a sudden clearing out of built-up toxins. An overdose can cause abdominal pain, diarrhea, and vomiting. I use precisely 1 drop in a 16-ounce glass of water for cleansing and 1 drop per gallon of water to eliminate contamination. If you are not familiar with this product, it is important that you request that the health food store or pharmacy provide you with an information sheet or that you check with your physician.

If you can't find food-grade hydrogen peroxide, you can boost the alkalinity of your water by adding ¼ teaspoon of baking soda per gallon for a short time (not on a regular basis). The goal is to neutralize acidity and help the body flush toxins. This process will help you eliminate harmful bacteria and maintain a stronger immune system that is essential for survival in a toxic environment.

Just because water is in a bottle doesn't mean it is healthful. When shopping for water, please read the label. If it says "drinking water," it usually is tap water filtered by methods such as reverse osmosis and then fortified. Read the label and avoid water that is treated and contains additives that can make the water harmful.

Avoid drinking tap water. It is exposed to many impurities and may contain harmful contaminants. Some of the contaminants include arsenic, asbestos, cyanide, E. coli and fecal coliform (bacteria), fluoride, lead, and mercury. The tap water is treated to reduce the contamination to minute quantities that are considered safe. However, consumption and accumulation of these toxins over a lifetime can increase the risk of cancer, birth defects, intestinal polyps, nerve damage, thyroid problems, attention span and learning disabilities, kidney problems, high blood pressure and bone disease. Your body has enough to deal with. Why add more contaminants, minute or otherwise?

For more information visit: *www.epa.gov/safewater/contaminants/index.html.*

If you still think that tap water is safe to drink, I ask you to consider the pipes that "purified" water must travel through before it gets to you. Corrosion of aging plumbing systems can be a source of lead contamination, and PVC pipes can be a breeding ground for bacteria.

For those who choose to drink distilled water. I understand that the distillation process purifies the water, but it also removes all of the natural elements like trace minerals. The distillation process renders the water low in particles. When it interacts with the bloodstream, which is high in particles, it absorbs your vital elements such as minerals and flushes them out. If you choose to consume distilled water, it is important to re-mineralize your body. To replenish my trace minerals, I use ¼ teaspoon of Real-Salt in an 8-ounce glass of water, as needed.

Dehydration occurs when you lose more fluid than you take in and your body doesn't have enough water and other fluids to carry out normal functions (like proper elimination). If it is hot out or you have been exercising and perspiring, drink more water to compensate. It's like filling your radiator! We need to consume 64 ounces per day or more depending on our activity level, the weather, and other factors including what we eat and drink. For example, alcohol is very dehydrating so we must drink at least 2 glasses of water for every alcoholic beverage consumed.

The chart below shows the minimum optimal daily consumption. Required intake will vary depending on level of activity, diet, exposure to heat or cold, humidity, and body fat. The more body fat you have, the more water you need.

DAILY WATER CONSUMPTION CHART

Age	Amount
0 to ½ year	4-6 ounces
½ to 1 year	16 ounces
1 to 3 years	24 ounces
3 to 7 years	32 ounces
7 to 13 years	48 ounces
13 to adult	64 ounces

living beyond organic

For a greater understanding about the properties of water, I recommend reading the illuminating work of Dr. Masaru Emoto: *The Hidden Messages in Water* and *The True Power of Water Healing and Discovering Ourselves.*

Herbal Tea Making and Brewing Instructions

Surprisingly, most Westerners are not familiar with the proper brewing of a healing cup or pot of tea. This is important because herbal teas' medicinal properties can be lost or evaporated if proper attention is not applied during preparation and storage. Tea can be used whenever flushing, calming, or neutralizing is required and is especially good for adding to baths to break fevers, cause a detoxifying sweat, absorb healing properties through the skin, or just to relax. The skin can absorb the medicinal properties of herbs in about 20 minutes.

Whenever possible, use freshly picked and dried herbs. Do not use tea bags as they can be infested with harmful molds, and bleached tea bags contaminate tea water with chlorine and other chemicals.

Select the Right Tea for Your Bathwater

- Thyme to break a fever
- Chamomile to cause a sweat, especially if sipped during the bath
- Sage to purify blood fluids through the skin, especially if sipped during the bath
- Goldenrod to purify the lymphatic fluids through the skin
- Peppermint to open constricted ducts and to stimulate appetite
- Ginger to stimulate circulation
- Arnica to soothe bruises
- Juniper berry to neutralize uric acids in skin tissues and joints

The two types of herbal teas require different methods of extracting their properties during the brewing process. These methods are known as infusion and decoction.

Infusion herbs are never boiled; their properties are released with just the application of boiled water. Infusion herbs are the tender leaves, flowers, soft stems, and berries. In either case, once the recently boiled water and the herbs make contact, the container needs to be covered immediately. The healing properties are contained within the essential oils of these herbs; when they are released they quickly dissipate through the steam. When the tea is brewed properly the oils can be seen floating on the surface. To enjoy the maximum benefit from your tea, keep it covered to save the essential oils from escaping. For best results drink within 20 minutes of brewing or store in an airtight, glass-lined stainless steel container.

Infusion (leaves, flowers, stems, and berries): Bring water to a boil, then remove from heat. Add ½ (half) a teaspoon of dried herb(s) per every cup of water boiled. Cover with airtight lid and steep for 15 to 30 minutes. The longer the herb steeps in water, the stronger the tea will be. Strain tea through unbleached cheesecloth or a stainless steel or porcelain strainer into the cup, and drink straight or sweetened, hot or cold, with raw honey, brown rice syrup or Grade B maple syrup, or Sucanat (sweeten when hot for proper dissolving).

A tea decoction is made with barks, roots, pods, and reeds. It needs to be boiled from 15 to 30 minutes, depending on the thickness or hardness of the herbal fiber. The essential oils of these herbs are not released until they have been simmered and well soaked.

Decoction (bark, root, and reed): Bring water to a boil in covered saucepan. Add ½ teaspoon of dried herb(s) per cup of boiling water. Replace cover and reduce heat to simmer. Continue simmering for 20 minutes and then steep for 20 minutes. The more herbs you use and the longer they steep in water, the stronger the tea will be. Strain tea through cheesecloth or a stainless-steel strainer into cup and drink straight or sweetened with raw honey or Grade B maple syrup. A decoction can be stored up to 12 hours in a stainless-steel thermos or glass pitcher with a tight-fitting lid. Please note that when drinking tea for the purpose of flushing toxins the tea is best unsweetened.

*Harmful bacteria
can thrive in an
acidic environment.
Be wise and alkalize!*

CHAPTER FOUR

Alkaline vs. Acid: The Goal is to Neutralize Acidity

WE NEED TO MAINTAIN OUR BODY'S NATURAL pH BALANCE. This balance is easily destroyed when we eat highly acidic refined or processed foods. The resulting acidic environment sustains harmful bacterial presence. Eating Super Enzyme Foods helps restore pH balance, which reduces harmful bacterial presence in the small intestine and colon.

Although pH balance is desirable, it is only one of many indicators of overall health. I have tested between 7 and 7.5 pH even when I had large amounts of old toxins present in my system.

- **What is pH?** Potential (p) of hydrogen (H) is a measure of the acidity or alkalinity of a solution. It is measured on a scale of 0 to 14. The lower the pH, the more acidic the solution; the higher the pH, the more alkaline (or basic) the solution. When a solution is neither acidic nor alkaline, it has a pH of 7, which is the goal for achieving healthy conditions.

- **Enzyme-depleted foods trigger increased hydrochloric acid production.** To compensate for the lack in enzymatic content, your stomach compromises the delicate internal balance of your entire body.

- **Pork, chicken, turkey, cow's milk/cheese, apples, oranges, bell peppers, peanut butter, celery, carrots, and yellow onions are some of the worst offenders.** Foods that are difficult to digest require enormous amounts of digestive juices and must wait until enough is present. This halt in the digestive process is far from benign. These acidic foods putrefy and release massive amounts of toxins, creating the perfect breeding ground for bacterial, viral, and fungal presence.

- **Toxicity/acidity makes you a ticking time bomb.** Your digestive system becomes a tumultuous, bacteria-riddled environment in which your organs must compete for survival. Food toxins pillage your body, lodging in the weakest organs, which break down the fastest under this attack. A toxic presence builds up and as the symptoms appear, the cause of the problem goes unrecognized. The name given to the disease is based on where the toxins are trapped.

- **Death starts in the colon.** Fluids are absorbed in the colon. This is where acidic conditions often generate a hostile environment for nutrients that have the potential to repair the damage. Your body is able to assimilate minerals and nutrients properly only when it is pH-balanced. It is therefore possible for you to take in healthy nutrients and yet be unable to absorb or use them. Nutrients destroyed by acidity simply produce more toxicity. These acidic conditions force the body to borrow minerals (including calcium, sodium, potassium, and magnesium) from vital organs and bones to buffer the acid and safely remove it from the body. Organs that readily provide vitamins and minerals from their reserves eventually deplete themselves. The colon is plunged into a state of turmoil as it struggles to defend its integrity despite the enormous amounts of toxicity sent to it by the rest of the body. The colon literally represents the last stand in this war against acidity and toxicity.

- **Recognize the need to alkalize.** Just as the colon can be a place of death, it can also be one of rebirth. Super Enzyme

Foods alkalize the digestive system and remove the toxic elements from the intestinal tract, thus balancing your pH level and restoring your health.

Harmful bacteria like E. coli and Streptococcus thrive in an acidic environment and can cause symptoms like diarrhea and sore throat. When we eat hard-to-digest foods—even raw foods that have high fiber content but low enzyme content such as celery, apples, and carrots—our body must produce more hydrochloric acid in the stomach. You can prevent this by switching to Super Enzyme alternatives like fennel bulb, pears, and raw yams. One of the most effective ways to counteract acidity is to prepare and drink the following:

- Potato water extract: Grate 1 medium red potato into 32 ounces of spring water; let it sit overnight at room temperature in an airtight glass dish. Strain, discard potato shreds, refrigerate, and drink potato water throughout the day.

Due to its enzymatic properties once the extract is ready it must be consumed within 24 hours.

Four Main Points to Consider

- **Life begins in the liver. It is the filter of the body**. Your body needs a clean filter to function properly. The liver is responsible for filtering all food you consume and all fluid in your body. Help keep it clean by avoiding rancid fatty foods that cause toxic buildup. Be sure to have olive oil, lemon, and crookneck squash regularly.

- **Kidneys filter the blood and all fluids** (blood fluids and lymphatic fluids) and send the waste to your bladder. Avoid drinking soda containing high fructose corn syrup or artificial sweeteners. Eat one cup of papaya and drink at least eight glasses of water daily.

- **The pancreas produces the insulin that balances sugar and all nutrients, provides alkalizing bile for digestion, produces hormones, and supports the immune system.** Avoid developing highly acidic conditions that result from over-consumption of highly processed dead foods. Instead, be sure to eat lots of red kidney beans and fresh raw salads.

- **A clogged colon forms from years of built-up toxins and undigested food**. The resulting acidity breeds bacteria and compromises your immunity, making you susceptible to dis-ease. Keep the colon clean by avoiding enriched white rice and flour, all refined sugar, pork, beef, and chicken. Instead, be sure to eat whole grains, raw nuts, and seeds daily.

"When a person's gastrointestinal system is clean, that person's body is easily able to fight off disease of whatever type."

—*The Enzyme Factor* Hiromi Shinya, M.D.

What's clogging your colon is what's killing you. Just as the liver is the source of life for the body, a clogged colon is the source of dis-ease. Residual undigested food gets stuck in the colon where it putrefies and acidifies. The colon lines its walls with mucous to protect itself, forming a mucoid plaque over time. As this condition develops, the colon becomes less effective in reclaiming water and eliminating waste. Impaction of feces along the colon walls traps toxicity in the body and promotes bacterial and viral presence. This degenerative cycle plunges the immune system into a critically weakened state which disables it from preventing a multitude of symptoms and illnesses.

The following bit of trivia may surprise you, but I think it's relevant to the poor condition of health in America.

The more bad fat in a food product, the longer it will stay in the body and putrefy. Bits of residue from the peanut butter and jelly sandwich on white bread that you ate years ago might still be there. Those potato chips you ate in elementary school might still be there. Your favorite pepperoni pizza from grad night may have taken up permanent residence. Fast-food burgers, tacos, and fried chicken might have mutated into alien life-forms. And that gyro with hummus or perhaps the carrots and creamy dip from your "healthy eating" phase are still hanging around (not to mention the toxins from plastic packaging and preservatives). If any of the above sounds familiar, there is a good chance that you will benefit from a colon cleanse. With that said, let's move on to white bread and why it is clogging your colon.

White bread is made from over-processed flour, which offers no real nutrients, is void of enzymes, and has been rendered indigestible. This means that white bread will be a burden on your digestive system and, ultimately, a disease-causing agent.

Peanut butter is made from the most fragile of all "nuts," but it's actually a legume. The enzymes and nutrients in peanuts break down within hours of harvesting and the oil becomes rancid. Refined sugar and salt are usually added, covering up the rancidity. Now the peanut butter is even more toxic. Since rancid fat, refined sugar, and refined salt cannot be used by the body, they get stored as toxins, which accumulate and can cause obesity and dis-ease.

Cow's milk, even organic cow's milk, is not the best source of calcium because the phosphorus in cow's milk inhibits calcium from being absorbed and used in humans. Additionally, we are all cow's milk-intolerant because the protein molecules are just too big to break down. Our body goes into protection mode and creates mucous to encapsulate these molecules. This leads to increased acidity, mucoid plaque buildup, bloating, constipation, congestion, and allergies.

> ## Do you want to COEXIST with old fecal matter, or are you ready to LET GO of it?

The effects of a colon cleanse are extremely detoxifying and rejuvenating. My husband completed a 21-day colon cleanse (refer to Appendix C). It consisted of raw foods such as nuts, seeds, salads, and vegetable blends. It wasn't easy, but he eliminated years of built-up toxins, increased his energy, and rejuvenated his appearance. Don't attempt this without a healthy liver strong enough to handle disposal of the toxins that will be dislodged by this rigorous cleanse.

By eating Super Enzyme Foods you gradually start the process of clearing out built-up toxins. Then, when you are ready, you can do an intense cleanse focusing on the colon. Always be sure to check with your health care practitioner first.

Ten Things that Will Help You De-Clog

1. **Drink more water**—improves elimination, flushes toxins, and keeps you looking youthful
2. **Eat half an avocado with two tablespoons of first cold-pressed extra virgin olive oil daily**—targets removal of rancid fat buildup
3. **Eat raw red potato**—alkalizes and helps with elimination
4. **Eat raw red beets**—helps eliminate harmful free radicals due to its high antioxidant properties
5. **Eat raw broccoli**—a good source of antioxidants and fiber
6. **INS wheatgrass powder**—with the root is a balanced, powerful antioxidant
7. **Drink Beyond Lemon Cleanse** (*see recipe on page 78*)— alkalizes, reduces bacteria, and boosts immunity
8. **Drink horsetail tea**—flushes toxins, reduces bloating
9. **Drink goat's milk**—digests easily, helps clean out colon
10. **Drink Papua New Guinea Coffee**—(*see recipe on page 180*) helps draw toxins into the colon to be eliminated

What to Expect

Soon after you begin the detoxification of built-up toxins, you may notice:
• Improved elimination
• Less bloating
• Reduced stomach acidity
• Improved mood
• Fewer headaches
• Less pain

After a few weeks, you may experience:
• Clearer thinking
• Better sleep patterns

- Enhanced sight, smell, and taste
- Better decision-making

Those who continue the process may feel:
- Calm, patient, and centered
- A return of positive feelings and thoughts
- A renewed desire to have fun
- More energy

As you eliminate toxins from your body and you begin to absorb more nutrients, you are on your way to feeling "super."

How Food Works for You

CARBOHYDRATES absorb vitamins

VITAMINS neutralize toxins and break down protein

PROTEINS digest fat

FATS absorb minerals

MINERALS restore immunity and maintain health—without minerals we cannot sustain life

When we understand that Super Enzyme Foods provide the nutrients the body needs and the enzymes necessary for proper digestion, we are motivated to pay attention to what we eat.

Carbohydrates absorb vitamins. Carbohydrates are a combination of carbon, hydrogen, and oxygen. Found in sugars and starches, the components of carbohydrates are quickly turned into immediate energy sources that enable cells to access vitamins. Carbohydrates found in fresh fruits begin the ideal digestive process. When we eat highly enzymatic fruits for breakfast, we give our body an enzymatic jumpstart for the whole day.

Good sources of carbohydrates from fruit include: papaya, pineapple, pear, avocado, raspberry, kiwi, peach, apricot, and plum. They are instant energy and vitality. They provide enzymes, vitamins, minerals, and essential oils for boosting organ function. On the other hand, low-enzyme foods like apples, oranges, grapefruit, bell peppers, and carrots can create swelling and acidity and intensify existing pain and constriction in the body.

Good sources of carbohydrates from grains are: organic whole unrefined grains, wheat, barley, corn, and brown rice. They provide super energy, vitamins, minerals, enzymes, and essential fatty acids, and they help maintain the quality of every organ function. Carbohydrates from refined, enriched white pastry flour, or enriched pasta and oats, promote cell death, intestinal impaction, acidity, toxicity, and organ damage.

High-enzyme starchy carbohydrates like red potatoes and yams (preferably raw) produce immediate and long-term energy units for every cell in the body, especially in the colon and sexual organs.

Vitamins neutralize toxins and break down protein. Vitamins are organic substances that regulate so many processes within your cells that virtually every action you perform requires their presence. Vitamins, together with amino acids and minerals, control cellular respiration, a process you need to live.

Water-soluble vitamins (Vitamin C, bioflavonoid and B-complex) are not stored; they travel through your bloodstream. What your body doesn't use, it simply excretes through urination. These vitamins need to be constantly replenished because your body can't hold on to them. Since excess vitamins are flushed out, it's difficult to overdose.

Fat-soluble vitamins are easily stored. Because these vitamins (A, D, E, and K) can stay in your body for a few days or as long as six months, in too large a quantity they can have a toxic presence and induce symptoms that are surprisingly similar to those caused by a deficiency of that vitamin.

Your body can't produce adequate vitamins under stress. Any form of stress inhibits your body's ability to make vitamins, particularly the B vitamins. Even if you were stress-free, your body could only produce some vitamins in minute amounts. The safest and surest way to provide your body with vitamins *that you* *can use* is through your daily intake of—you've guessed it—Super Enzyme Foods. In addition, daily supplementation of a food-based B-complex is essential, especially if you are under stress.

For good food and herb sources of vitamins (preferably eaten in their organic, fresh, raw state), refer to Appendix A. I found this information helpful in my healing process and recommend it for those who want more information.

Proteins digest fat. A complete protein contains nine essential amino acids. Proteins access the body through foods that are complete proteins unto themselves and from combinations of foods. A complete protein combination contains nine or more amino acids. A *complete whole protein* such as meat provides nutrients for specific organ functions. A *complete protein combination* such as brown rice and red kidney beans provides nutrients that can be used wherever they are needed in the body. It is a good idea to provide your body with complete protein combinations in addition to whole proteins on a regular basis to ensure that you are getting enough nutrients for all your organs so that they can function effectively. Ideally, a good protein source is easily digestible, completely usable, and alkalizing, and it provides the body with amino acids.

Good protein sources are goat's milk, cheese, and yogurt; sheep's milk, cheese, and yogurt; brown rice and red kidney beans (combined); bison meat; wild salmon; organic tofu; raw almonds and cashews (including their milk); wild orange roughy; wild lake trout; and sprouted grains and seeds.

Bad protein sources are indigestible, will cause acidity, and if not eliminated will putrefy, form gas, and contribute to the deterioration of your immune system. They include chicken, pork, cow's milk, cow's cheese, beef, peanuts, oats, turkey, lamb, walnuts, pecans, white rice, garbanzo beans, and pinto beans.

Fats absorb minerals. The major misconception about fats is that all fats are bad. Let's clarify this. There is good fat and there is bad fat. Good fats are a source of the good cholesterol that helps keep your brain cells functioning, your nerves able to conduct electrical communications, your liver making digestive bile, and your skin converting sunlight to vitamin D (the main immune system vitamin). Bad fats are toxic and contribute to slow

alkaline vs. acid

poisoning of the colon, skin, nerves, arteries, and fatty tissues, impairing the function of all organs.

Some good fats are almonds, almond butter, Brazil nuts, coconut, coconut oil and butter, flax seeds, goat's cheese and butter, hemp seeds, hemp oil, organic unsalted butter (from cow's milk), sesame seeds, sesame oil, and sunflower seeds.

Some bad fats are shortening (which is life-shortening), closely followed by margarine and congealed animal fats (especially lard from pork), and refined and partially hydrogenated vegetable oils. Most commercial grade potato or corn chips, French fries, and mass-produced pastries and doughnuts with few exceptions have been made with bad fats to increase their shelf life. And you can bet these fats will putrefy and store themselves inside your body. They're harmful, and you need to know about them so that you can make better choices.

Two Kinds of Fats

The two different types of fats are fatty acids and essential fatty acids (EFAs). Fatty acids can be produced by the body. However, essential fatty acids are not produced by the body and must be supplied in your daily food. The only two foods that contain every essential fatty acid are, as I hope you know by now, AVOCADOS and FIRST COLD-PRESSED EXTRA VIRGIN OLIVE OIL.

One of the best sources of good fat is organic first cold-pressed (FCP) extra virgin olive oil (preferably from France, Italy, Greece, or Spain) because it is minimally processed and contains EFAs your body needs. Olive oil contains oleic acid, which helps prevent plaque buildup in the arteries. Another key Super Enzyme Food is the avocado, preferably organic. Avocados contain lipoic acid and are richer in vitamin E than any other fruit, which makes them powerful free-radical scavengers. Together, avocados and olive oil create a dynamic duo that will help you win the battle against rancid fat buildup. By eating half an avocado and 2 tablespoons of FCP olive oil daily, you provide the liver with proper cholesterols that in turn enable the body to remove harmful cholesterol. They also use vitamin C to repair vessel damage, vitamins A and E to neutralize any oxidation and free radicals, and vitamin D to boost the immune system. Most important, this combination can help you dissolve old, rancid fat deposits in the body.

Surprisingly, other good fat sources are organic heavy cream and organic unsalted butter (in moderation). Both of these are a great source of conjugated linoleic acid (CLA), a beneficial component of the omega-6 fatty acid family. Studies by scientists from Harvard Medical School have revealed CLA's anti-carcinogenic properties, which include inhibiting tumor growth and proliferation of human cancer cells. Found primarily in meat and dairy products, CLA has Super Enzyme sources, which include grass-fed bison, organic heavy cream, and organic unsalted butter (cow's dairy, but not to be confused with cow's milk products).

Minerals restore immunity and maintain health. Without minerals, we cannot sustain life. Many large-scale farmers grow food in mineral-depleted soil, producing a mineral-deprived harvest. Organic foods contain more minerals than food grown in synthetically amended soils, but your best choice is food grown at home or purchased from farmers' markets where food has been grown in composted soil or in re-mineralized soil with the use of red worm castings.

Living organisms cannot make minerals; they are elements that originate in the earth. Most of the minerals in our diets come directly from plants or indirectly from animal sources. There are two kinds of minerals: macro-minerals and trace minerals. Macro minerals include organic calcium, magnesium, phosphorus, potassium, sodium, and sulfur. We need smaller amounts of trace minerals such as cobalt, copper, iodine, iron, manganese, selenium, and zinc.

For good food and herb sources, refer to Appendix B.

The following are complete foods because they contain all five categories of nutrients:

- Avocado
- Goat's milk
- Mango
- Carob powder
- Buckwheat

Remember: the presence of enzymes makes all the functions of the body possible.

What your BODY can't use or ELIMINATE, it will STORE.

When we consume more food than our body can use, or when we eat food that our body cannot digest, the following problems may result:

- **Excess calories** from unusable toxic sources are stored in fatty tissue. This causes fat cells to enlarge, leading to obesity.
- **Excess inorganic minerals** such as synthetic calcium supplements and iodized sodium can cause mucus and calcification, which can lead to arthritis.
- **Unusable protein** from chicken, turkey, and beef mutates cells and can lead to cancer and other abnormal growths.
- **Indigestible rancid fats** from hydrogenated oils and toxic animal fat build up in the blood and can lead to vessel plaque and high cholesterol.
- **Indigestible refined sugar**, such as refined cane, beet, and especially high fructose corn syrup, builds up in the blood and can lead to diabetes.

Free Enzymes and Digestive Enzyme Supplements

The bad news is that enzymes are destroyed at 118 degrees Fahrenheit within 30 minutes. This means we need to eat 60 percent of our meal raw. And, as we age, the need for exogenous enzymes increases.

Remember when you could eat anything and not gain weight? Well, that's because when we were young, we had high enzyme potential. As we age we deplete the enzyme potential, and the need for raw foods and enzyme supplements increases. It is best to derive your enzymes from eating raw foods with every cooked meal; when that is not possible, digestive enzyme supplements help. The use of digestive enzyme supplements with cooked foods improves digestion but is not a substitute for raw foods.

Supplementation eases digestion, allowing metabolic enzymes to continue their intended metabolic functions. As a result you will:

- Improve digestion of cooked foods
- Improve assimilation of nutrients
- Improve elimination
- Let go of excess weight
- Increase your energy level

Although the enzymes of many raw foods are "locked," i.e., bound to their nutrients and will break down only their own nutrients, there are some raw foods that contain unlocked enzymes. The good news is that we can eat cooked food (not overcooked or processed) and still absorb nutrients by combining the following "free enzyme" raw foods:

- Avocado
- Mango
- Papaya
- Peach
- Pear
- Persimmon
- Pineapple
- Plum
- Pomegranate
- Prune
- Red beet

By including these foods in your meals, you will achieve improved digestion and nutrient absorption. However, sometimes the body needs a boost. For best results, I supplement with digestive enzymes, especially for weight loss, as needed.

After learning about digestive enzyme supplements, I found that the source of the enzyme is just as important as the potency. Enzymes from a plant source are best at providing a combination of protease, lipase, amylase, and lactase.

I found that even though I was eating raw foods—perhaps not enough—I had reached a plateau in my weight loss, and when I started taking digestive enzyme supplements with my cooked food, I was able to let go of excess weight.

Living Beyond Organic
Try it. What have
you got to lose?

C H A P T E R   F I V E

The Super Enzyme Challenge

SUPER ENZYME FOODS INCLUDE:

- **Herbs** that neutralize, repair, and heal organs
- **Foods and fats** that boost and energize the function of hormones
- **Organic (from a food source) vitamins** that detoxify organs and systems
- **Organic minerals** that restore and maintain immunity

I challenge you to eat solely from the Super Enzyme Foods list on page 38 for 21 days. You might be thinking: "Great. It worked for her and her family—but will it work for me?" Don't take my word for it. Eat exclusively from the Super Enzyme Foods list for 21 days and see for yourself. If it is not on the list, DO NOT eat it, period. After 21 days, try eating something you used to eat that is not on the list. Your body will know the difference. Many people who take the challenge seriously and adhere to it experience a dramatic change in their tolerance for foods they used to eat.

It is very important that we keep our priorities straight. If you are concerned with weight loss, remember that your health comes first! While being "skinny" doesn't necessarily equate to healthy; once you are Living Beyond Organic, reaching your optimum weight should come naturally. Bear in mind that as you cleanse your body and your palate, you will develop a new awareness and appreciation for foods that are good for you.

Carry the list that follows when you go shopping until its contents have become second nature. Be advised that although this is the list that we used to achieve our results, we make adjustments periodically. A current list of Super Enzyme Foods is available online at: *www.LivingBeyondOrganic.com.*

SUPER ENZYME FOODS

Vegetables

Artichoke	Leek	Tomato
Arugula	Lettuce	*(Roma,*
Asparagus	*(butter, endive,*	*Heirloom)*
Avocado	*radicchio, baby*	Watercress
Beets *(red)*	*spring mix)*	Yam
Broccoli	Kale	
Capers	Mushroom	
Cauliflower	*(chanterelle,*	
Crookneck squash	*crimini, porcini,*	
(yellow)	*reishi, shiitake)*	
Cucumber	Mustard greens	
Eggplant	Onion *(red)*	
Fennel	Potato *(red)*	
Horseradish	Spinach	
Jicama	Swiss chard	

Sprouts

Alfalfa	Buckwheat	Red clover
Bean *(mung)*	Fenugreek	Sunflower
Broccoli	Mustard seed	Wheat

Grains

Amaranth	Kamut	Rice
Barley	Millet	*(basmati,*
Buckwheat		*brown, wild)*
Corn *(organic)*		Wheat

Berries

Bilberry	Gooseberry	Mulberry
Blackberry	Hawthorne berry	Raspberry
Boysenberry	Juniper berry	Red currant
Cranberry	Loganberry	Strawberry

Fish/Meat

Lake trout	Shrimp *(jumbo)*	Bison/buffalo
Orange roughy	*(All above must be*	*(organic,*
Salmon	*wild caught)*	*grass-fed*
		preferred)

Fruits

Apricot	Guava	Peach
Banana	Honeydew melon	Pear
(after five hours	Kiwi	Persimmon
of sunlight)	Lemon	Pineapple
Cantaloupe	Lime	Plum
Cherry	Mandarin orange	Pomegranate
Coconut	Mango	Prune
Date	Nectarine	Star fruit
Fig	Olives	Tangerine
Grape	Papaya	
(red, blue, black)	Passion fruit	

Herbs/Spices

Allspice	Dill	Paprika
Anise	Fenugreek	Peppermint
Basil	Garlic *(elephant)*	Rosemary
Bay leaf	Ginger	Sage
Cayenne	Hawthorne leaf	Spearmint
Chamomile	Marigold flowers	Tarragon
Chives	Marjoram	Thyme
Cilantro	Mustard *(seed, leaf)*	Turmeric
Cinnamon	Noni	Vanilla bean
Cloves	Nutmeg	Yucca
Cumin	Oregano	

Miscellaneous

Beer *(Coors Light)*	Noni juice *(pure)*	Vinegars
Brewers' yeast	Red wine	*(balsamic,*
Carob	*(aged seven*	*brown rice,*
Chocolate *(dark)*	*years or more)*	*plum, red wine)*
Coffee	Sake *(unfiltered)*	Vodka
(Papua New	Sea salt	*(Absolut)*
Guinea)	*(unrefined*	
Duck eggs	*RealSalt brand)*	
Honeycomb *(raw)*	Tofu *(organic)*	

Natural Sweeteners

Brown rice syrup	Honey *(raw)*	Molasses
Date sugar	Maple syrup	Sucanat
Fructose	*(Grade B)*	
(unrefined)		

Beans

Anasazi	Lentils *(red)*	White (Cannellini,
Edamame	Lima	Great Northern,
Green	Soybean	Navy)
Kidney *(dark red)*		

Milk Products

Almond milk
Buffalo/bison's milk,
cheese, yogurt
Butter
*(organic,
unsalted cow's)*
Coconut milk
Feta cheese
*(from the goat
or sheep)*

Goat's butter,
cheese, milk,
yogurt
Heavy whipping
cream
(organic cow's)
Rice milk *(organic)*
Sheep's milk
or cheese

Sour cream,
crème fraîche
*(100% cream
only; Daisy
brand)*
Soy milk *(organic)*

Nuts/Seeds

Almond
Anise seed
Brazil nut
Caraway seed

Cashews
Fennel seed
Flaxseed
Pine nut

Sesame seed
Sunflower seed

Excellent Protein Sources

Almond
Almond milk
Avocado
Beans
*(Anasazi,
Cannellini,
Great Northern,
kidney, Navy,
soy)*

Feta
*(sheep or
goat's milk)*
Goat's milk,
cheese, yogurt
Grain
*(especially
whole wheat
and wheat
sprouts)*
Lentil *(red)*

Mushroom
Potato *(red)*
Rice milk
Romano cheese
*(from sheep's
milk)*
Sprouts
Soy milk
Tofu *(organic)*
Whole wheat pasta

Excellent Essential Fatty Acids Sources

Avocado
Cashews
Feta cheese
(sheep's milk)

Goat's milk,
cheese, yogurt
Grain
*(especially
wheat)*

Olives
Romano cheese
(sheep's milk)
Soy milk
Sunflower seed

Oils (cold pressed, expeller pressed, and extra virgin)

Apricot kernel	Flaxseed	Safflower
Avocado	Grape seed	Sunflower
Coconut	Olive *(extra virgin)*	Wheat germ

High-Heat Oils for Cooking

Coconut	Safflower	Sunflower
Corn *(organic)*	Sesame seed	

Oils for Raw Use Only

Almond	Flaxseed	Olive *(extra virgin)*
Apricot kernel	Grape seed	Soy *(organic)*
Avocado	Hemp	Vitamin E

Foods to Avoid

Apple
Artificial
    sweeteners
Bell pepper
Canola oil
Carrots
Celery
Coffee
    (except Papua
    New Guinea)
Cow's dairy
    products
    (except organic
    heavy cream, or-
    ganic unsalted
    butter, and
    colostrum)

Chicken eggs
Crab
Garlic *(regular)*
Grapefruit
Hot peppers
    (except cayenne
    and Anaheim)
Iceberg lettuce
Lobster
Oats
Onions
    (yellow, white)
Oranges
Peanuts
Pecans
Pepper
    (black and
    white)

Pistachios
Pork products
Pumpkin seeds
Rye
Shark
Soft drinks
Squash
    (except
    crookneck)
Sugar
    (over-processed)
Sweet potato
Tuna
Walnuts
Watermelon
White flour
White rice

Your Cheat Sheet

This is a quick reference of foods that are simple to replace and that will make a big difference.

Replace:	With:
Tap water	Natural spring water bottled at source
Iodized salt	RealSalt
Black pepper	Cayenne pepper
Processed sugar	Sucanat, raw wild honey, brown rice syrup, Grade B maple syrup, black strap molasses, date sugar, unrefined corn fructose
Cow's milk, cheese, and yogurt	Goat's milk and cheese, water buffalo cheese, sheep's milk and cheese, bison's milk, cheese, and yogurt
Pork, beef, chicken, turkey, and lamb	Bison, wild-caught salmon, orange roughy, lake trout, and jumbo shrimp
Apples and oranges	Pears and tangerines
Enriched white bread/pasta/rice	Whole grain bread/pasta and brown rice
Peanut butter	Cashew/almond butter, organic soy or hemp butter, sunflower seed butter
Soft drinks	Organic root beer, ginger beer
Cooking with olive oil	Cooking with safflower oil

Food Characteristics and Nutrition

Good nutrition consists of foods that:

- Are rich in enzymes
- Are alkalizing
- Can be digested and absorbed
- Help clear out toxins

Super Enzyme Foods work synergistically to supply energy and nutrients to your body and, most important, help your digestive system. Super Enzyme Foods have four main characteristics:

- High in enzymatic content
- Highly alkalizing
- High in digestible nutritive components
- Boost organ function

When you eat foods that are low in enzymes, your pancreas is unable to produce enough alkalizing enzymes and degenerates. Your liver makes slimy digestive bile, and your colon sandwiches food toxins into layers of mucus on its walls.

It is important for you to know that many foods that are high in nutrients don't have enough accompanying enzymes to utilize these nutrients. During digestion, these foods stress the organs.

In my cooking classes, I compare a pear and an apple. Each has fiber and nutrients, but the pear contains enough enzymes to digest itself, as is evidenced by its short shelf life. The apple, which is comparatively low in enzymes, has a much longer shelf life. That's probably why you see so many varieties of apples and so few pears in the markets.

Watermelon is an example of high sugar/low enzyme relationship. Although watermelon has high lycopene content, it is difficult for the body to access it due to the fruit's low enzyme content. In addition, watermelon's diuretic properties combined with its lack of minerals can leach the minerals out of your body.

Blueberries also have a high nutrient/low enzyme relationship. Although blueberries are high in antioxidants, they are low in the enzymes necessary for optimum digestion and assimilation of those nutrients.

Food Axioms

The following reveals the truth about axioms that for years I thought were true but now know are generally accepted misinformation.

- **An apple a day keeps the doctor in pay.**
  An apple is so low in enzymes and so acidic that it exacerbates every pain and swelling process in the body. This also applies to apple juice.

- **Oranges are not good for you.**
  An orange is so acidic that your body must encapsulate it in mucus to try to remove it from every detoxification channel, causing all kinds of allergies. This is also true for orange juice.

- **All carotene is not equal.**
  The carotene in carrots produces an extra enzyme complex in the liver that inhibits certain functions, forcing detoxification through the skin and at toxic levels, resulting in abnormal skin pigmentation. This is also true for carrot juice.

- **The detriments of bell peppers far outweigh the benefits.**
  Bell peppers of all colors create a harmful bacterial environment in the small intestine. The bacteria on the hands of produce handlers thrive on the pepper skin and continue to grow even after cooking. The worst case of food poisoning I ever had was from a ham and cheese sandwich with roasted bell pepper.

- **Black pepper is bad.**
  Even though it is antibacterial, black pepper is one of the most dangerous foods for the liver. Over time it can cause more scar tissue than alcoholism.

- **Oats have an acidic effect.**
  They are great for horses but are not for human consumption. They are highly acidic. I know that this is shocking for most people to hear, especially those eating it for health. I ate oatmeal for breakfast for years. It wasn't my favorite, but I thought I was eating healthfully. I loved granola bars made of oats and lots of refined sugar. I also suffered with acid indigestion regularly. I now use rolled barley instead. It has alkalizing properties

that make it much easier to digest and can be used in place of oatmeal in your favorite recipes.

- **Low-fat/nonfat dairy is not better for you.**
  Cow milk products need to be avoided. They cause acidity, are indigestible, and inhibit brain function. When fat or total fat is removed from milk protein, you've removed the only part that is beneficial. It is the milk's protein that is not usable. It increases mucous production and contributes to plaque build-up in the colon. Instead, use regular goat's milk, sheep's milk, or buffalo/bison milk and cheese which provide the body with nutrition and healing properties. Exceptions to cow dairy are organic heavy cream and organic unsalted butter, because these fats can be used and digested to support body function.

*If you want
to feel better,
perhaps it's time
to make the switch.*

C H A P T E R   S I X

Super Enzyme Foods Frequently Asked Questions

EATING BEYOND ORGANIC MEANS STICKING TO THE SUPER ENZYME Foods list for at least 21 days. Once you have determined that you feel better and want to Live Beyond Organic, I will teach you how to deal with situations in which occasional deviation from the list is unavoidable. But until you detoxify, sticking to the list is the only way to get results. My primary goal is to teach you how you can be healthy and eat delicious meals too!

Why wild-caught salmon?

Wild-caught salmon are rich in long-chain omega-3 fatty acids and antioxidants that help lower the risk of heart disease and cancer. The wild Alaskan species grow free of antibiotics, pesticides, and synthetic coloring agents, and they have the least amount of mercury of almost any fish. Their coloring (beta carotene/vitamin A) comes from a natural diet and swimming free, which enables their hormone system to develop. But most important, this fish offers healthful nutrition for the human body, especially the nervous system.

Can I eat farm-raised salmon?

I avoid farm-raised salmon. It is an artificial organism genetically modified through synthetically enriched pellet feed. Its cells are abnormal and do not provide digestible vitamins and minerals. Instead they become like the pellets they consume and can serve only to genetically modify the human body. *Science Journal* warned that farm-raised salmon has ten times more toxins than wild-caught, which poses cancer risks to humans. These toxins can include PCBs, antibiotics, artificial coloring, and Calicide, which is used to kill parasites.

Why only jumbo shrimp?

Although shrimp are bottom feeders, jumbo shrimp (16 to 20 per pound) have a developed digestive system that enables the elimination of toxins such as mercury and other heavy metals. They are easily digested and a good source of protein, and they are beneficial for the spinal cord nerves. Some of the best are trap-caught jumbo shrimp, including pink, brown, white, and freshwater.

Why is orange roughy good?

Orange roughy is one of the most easily digestible deep water fish. It is rich in minerals, calcium, magnesium, and potassium, and it contains high amounts of silica, which enables the liver to regenerate filtering capability, boosts thyroid function, and is second only to eating salmon with the bones (all types of wild-caught salmon). In recipes like salmon cakes, salmon salad, or salmon loaf, the soft bones can be ground with the fish.

Why is lake trout good?

Lake trout depend on cold, oxygen-rich water to survive; this environment stimulates the production of omega-3. Deep-water trout can contain up to three times as much omega-3 as salmon. They are also a good source of protein, niacin, B12, pantothenic acid, and selenium. They are healing and they help to regenerate RNA.

Why not chicken?

Chicken is not a Super Enzyme Food. It is difficult to digest and putrefies in your intestines. It contains hormones that cause hormonal imbalance and, in greater concentrations, lead to a host of health risks. Chicken has been highly mutated. Even free-range organic chicken has been affected by years of genetic mutation.

What about chicken eggs?

The protein in chicken eggs is indigestible and has an acidic effect on the body. The best alternative is duck eggs because they are purely digestible, have more nutritional value, and are not subjected to genetic modification.

What about bacon or ham?

A good rule of thumb is that anything made from pork is an emphatic NO! Pork is riddled with a host of harmful parasites. Pigs eat parasites and store toxins in their flesh. Contrary to popular belief, all parasites are not destroyed during cooking, so if you eat pork, it is the same as eating toxic waste.

What about turkey breast?

For the most part turkey protein is indigestible and causes fermentation and harmful yeast growth in the small intestine.

Can I have something not on the list once in a while?

To answer this, I use a personal story. Tuna is not on the list. I craved tuna sushi and would eat it occasionally while I continued detoxifying. But once I had detoxified my body, tuna sushi tasted terrible to me. I haven't eaten it since. Overall, the desire for unhealthful foods diminishes.

What about a lapse from Super Enzyme Foods?

Yes, this often occurs, and if you have been on the Super Enzyme Foods list for at least 21 days your body will probably react adversely depending on the particular food and quantity eaten. Try to neutralize potential toxins with a restaurant survival kit and supplement with a glass of goat's milk with 25 drops of sarsaparilla extract (universal antidote for food poisoning).

Why isn't cabbage on the list?

Cabbage is not a Super Enzyme Food, and its diuretic properties strip minerals from the body. Furthermore, it must completely ferment to be digested, which causes bloating. This includes pickled cabbage.

Why can't I have zucchini?

Zucchini, like all other squash (except crookneck) has extremely low enzymes and stresses the liver and pancreas. Zucchini can cause loss of energy and equilibrium.

Are Gogi berries all right?

There are better choices such as concord grapes, dark cherries, and cranberries.

What is bison? I thought it was called buffalo.

Bison are indigenous to North America while the water buffalo is indigenous to India. Although we use both names in this country, the correct one is bison.

Where do you buy bison?

You can order it online or find it at specialty grocery stores and, increasingly, major supermarkets and some large discount stores. (Look for organic, grass-fed quality.) It is comparable in price to premium quality beef.

Does bison taste like beef?

Bison tastes better! If you like the taste of beef, you will love the taste of bison. I never made anything out of beef that doesn't taste better made with bison. However, for tenderness, most cuts of bison require marination.

Where can I find goat's milk?

Most specialty markets and grocery stores carry it these days.

How does goat's milk taste?

Delicious! When first starting out on Super Enzyme Foods, some people may have sensitivity to the taste of goat's milk. As they detoxify, their taste buds will adjust and appreciate it.

Is there a substitute for goat's milk?

No. However, when starting on Super Enzyme Foods, you can use organic rice milk, organic almond milk, or organic soy milk. Although they are not as beneficial as goat's milk, they will not promote toxic buildup like cow's milk. It is important to note that soy milk is a high source of estrogen, and an overabundance of estrogen can be harmful.

Can I feed my baby goat's milk?

Yes. In fact, goat's milk is the next best thing to healthy mother's milk. For a natural baby formula mix:

4 oz goat's milk
½ teaspoon brown rice syrup
¼ teaspoon carob powder

What is elephant garlic, and why should I use it instead of regular garlic?

Elephant garlic is a member of the leek family and has a milder flavor than regular garlic. Regular garlic has potent antibiotic properties, and eating it every day may be like taking prescription antibiotics regularly, killing both friendly and unfriendly bacteria. Elephant garlic allows you to enjoy the flavor of garlic without aftereffects such as garlic breath and body odor.

How do I eat in a restaurant?

I look for wild-caught salmon, jumbo shrimp, orange roughy, or lake trout. Avoid selections made with sauces. Use fresh squeezed lemon instead. I order an assortment of steamed or raw vegetables, baby mixed greens, arugula, or spinach salad with goat's cheese if available. I request that my food be steamed or grilled. I always travel with my own herb blend, FCP olive oil, RealSalt, cayenne pepper, and Sucanat (the *Living Beyond Organic* restaurant survival kit) to ease digestion and neutralize any rancid oil, processed salt, and black pepper or sugar that might find its way onto my plate. But, remember that this is for those unavoidable occasions, because if you are neutralizing bad food with good, you are stagnating instead of restoring health and rejuvenating. After eating out, I usually drink a glass of goat's milk with sarsaparilla extract when I get home to help neutralize any toxicity.

What do you do when you travel?

I call my hotel ahead of time, explain that I have special dietary requirements, and fax a copy of the Super Enzyme Foods list. I also look for local vegetarian restaurants (they usually serve whole grains and organic produce) and farmers' markets (for fresh produce). For convenience, I ship the bare necessities (available at *www.LBOrganic.com*) ahead of time to my destination.

What about airline food?

The best choice is to take something on board such as organic trail mix, crackers, cheese, flat bread roll-up sandwiches, and fruit. You can also call ahead. Airlines frequently have vegetarian selections, or you can request fruit.

What do you do when you go to a party?

If I don't know the host or hostess well, I eat something before I go, just in case. But friends are usually happy to accommodate you.

Specifics about Bison, Fiber, Salt, Sugar, Yeast, Gluten, and Lactose

Bison

Bison is not genetically modified; it is purely digestible and leaner than beef, which is why it requires marination or hydration. Bison does not produce the specific adrenaline that would cause all of the cellular vitality to go to specific organs, robbing other cells of energy. This process is known as "fight or flight." Therefore, it does not trigger catabolic steroid production in the kidney adrenals. Complex catabolic steroids contribute to breakdown of muscle tissue in humans. This condition may be caused by consumption of beef and lamb or being subjected to extreme/chronic stress, acidity, and poor diet.

Bison contains friendly parasites that break down the meat and leave with the waste. Pork, chicken, turkey, beef, and lamb (listed in descending order of contamination level) contain some parasites that are not destroyed during cooking and may take up permanent residence in your body.

Bison has a beneficial fat content of omega-3 fatty acids and conjugated linoleic acid (CLA) that have been shown to lower cholesterol levels. It is also high in iron. In addition to being leaner than most other meats, bison contains no growth hormones, steroids, or subtherapeutic antibiotics. Bison also helps remove stored deposits of rancid putrefied meats.

In addition, bison is an excellent food source of vitamin B12, which is necessary for proper digestion, absorption of foods, synthesis of protein, and metabolism of carbohydrates and fats. B12 is also linked to the production of acetylcholine, a neurotransmitter that assists memory and learning.

I prepare bison for my family up to three times per week. Bison can be used in any recipe that calls for beef, pork, or lamb. You won't compromise on flavor. Five years ago we made bison our meat of choice and have been enjoying the healthy benefits with our meals ever since. My husband's cholesterol level has never been better. My daughters and I are slender and energetic. What have you got to lose, except maybe stored toxins and excess weight? Try it and see for yourself.

Fiber comes in two forms:

Soluble (dissolves in water) and *insoluble* (doesn't dissolve in water). Barley and cauliflower are examples of soluble fiber, while fennel and asparagus are insoluble. High-fiber foods such as red lentils and dark red kidney beans are beneficial because their soluble portions are digested slowly. Although fiber is technically a carbohydrate, it has no digestible calories. So, the "low-carb" tortilla that is labeled 11 grams of carbohydrates (of which 8 grams are fiber) actually contains only 3 grams of usable carbohydrates that raise enough sugar for fuel while the rest are stored as bulk and fat in the colon. Therefore, "low-carb" is not necessarily better for you, whereas combining complex sugars slows down carbohydrate digestion, the key to preventing harmful surges of insulin.

Soluble fiber helps to remove cholesterol buildup in the blood by causing new bile to be made in the liver and preventing "recycling" of the bile. Cholesterol is taken from the bloodstream and used by the liver as the primary ingredient to make digestive bile. Cholesterol exchange is also what keeps the brain healthy.

It is equally important to eat "good" insoluble fiber, such as broccoli, crookneck squash, organic corn (popcorn too), and mango, because it helps keep food moving through the intestines and cleans intestinal and colon walls. "Empty" insoluble fiber such as apples, celery, and bell pepper are all low-enzyme foods and cause bloating, fermentation, acidity, and toxins.

Grains are also misunderstood. Years ago, I thought that rice was a starchy carb. The truth is that *white* rice is a starchy carb suitable for wallpaper paste, but organic brown rice is a great source of fiber, protein, amino acids, and vitamin E—a natural antioxidant.

What is the difference between regular sea salt and iodized table salt?

Regular sea salt is spoiled from the start because much of it is harvested from oceans exposed to environmental pollution and because it is evaporated in a potentially polluted environment. Iodized table salt is bleached and fortified with iodine (potassium iodide), a chemical substance used in photography in the preparation of silver iodide for high speed photographic film. This is the kind of salt that is extremely hazardous to your health. Even the iodine that you think you're getting is synthesized and destroys electrolytes and depletes minerals and therefore may cause fluid retention, high blood pressure, and other related dis-ease. RealSalt, however, is good for you. RealSalt is in its organic state and has all its minerals intact. Using regular sea salt, even organic, is not enough. RealSalt is a very specific product. It is mined from an ancient dead sea—not from a sea subjected to environmental toxins.

It is the antithesis of the impure salt product that damages your kidneys. RealSalt helps your kidneys to pH balance your blood fluids while normalizing blood pressure. It eliminates fluid retention in tissues by flushing out toxins. It boosts liver and all major organ functions and infuses your body with trace minerals. RealSalt wears many hats in my house; we:

- Use it in recipes for flavor and to re-mineralize foods
- Bathe in it to detoxify and as a mineral infusion
- Mix it in natural spring water to balance electrolytes instead of ingesting high-sugar sports drinks
- Gargle with it to help clear out built-up toxins
- Make a saline solution eye wash

An excellent source of organic sodium, RealSalt is a key to alkalizing, detoxifying, and rejuvenating your whole body. After all, every ounce of your lymphatic and blood fluid is saline-based.

> # Getting the human BODY to run on oil instead of SUGAR is like trying to get a diesel engine to RUN on gas.

Sugar

Think that to be truly healthy you have to give up sugar? Think again!

We need sugar to function. That is why fruit is so important and is the best carbohydrate!

Sugar, or sucrose, is the energy unit for every process and enzyme activity in the human body. The question is: What sugar is usable by the body and not a harmful toxin?

The *right* type of sugar will sustain energy without drop-offs, provide true fuel for cell function, sustain metabolic activity, help immune system organs produce lymphocyte "killer cells" that protect from antibody attacks, and support brain neural-net and nerve response. Some sugars also provide vitamins and minerals for proper metabolic use and balanced energy. Preferred sources are organic fresh fruit; minimally processed sugars such as Sucanat (dehydrated cane juice with no additives or preservatives); raw wild honey (unheated); unrefined fructose, a.k.a. fruit sugar (not from high fructose corn syrup), also Grade B or C maple syrup; and organic brown rice syrup. All are good sources of sugar when used in moderation.

I use Sucanat in my coffee, Grade B maple syrup in my smoothies, organic brown rice syrup on whole wheat English muffins, unrefined crystalline fructose (not high fructose corn syrup) in my organic whipped cream, and raw wild honey as a tea sweetener in a multitude of recipes and as a topical treatment for burns. I have not given up my sweet tooth. Instead, I choose to use healthy sweeteners in moderation.

> The **AVERAGE** American consumes **52 teaspoons** of refined **SUGAR** per day.

The *wrong* type of sugar debilitates digestive organ function, causes hormones to crash, causes critical insulin surges to store fat in tissue and triglycerides in blood vessels, interrupts nerve function and brain activity, depletes and suppresses immunity, and quickly turns to harmful acid.

ANY refined sugar is the wrong type of sugar, creating a fast burn and quick drop-off, leaving the body with no energy to use nutrients that accompany food. And while the body becomes starved for these missing nutrients, the wrong sugar, such as high fructose corn syrup, leaves behind unusable, putrefied waste.

You want to avoid refined cane and beet sugar, high fructose corn syrup, and heat-treated honey. They have been stripped of enzymes and nutrients by heat and over-processing.

Refined sugar is a poison to the human body and acts like a drug rather than a food. The process of refining removes all of sugar cane's natural minerals and vitamins, changes its ability to be used as fuel, and causes uncontrollable energy swings. Refined sugar hides in nearly every packaged, canned, boxed, and jarred convenience food. It lurks in salad dressings, ketchup, and concentrated fruit juice. The combined refined sugar content in meals composed of these products increases health risks. Don't get caught in this digestive stimulant/letdown cycle. Choose the right type of sugar for your health.

Artificial sweeteners: Aspartame is the generic name for branded artificial sweeteners such as NutraSweet, Equal Spoonful, and Equal Measure. It is one of the main ingredients in diet sodas and is sure to result in the dehydration of all your cells. Aspartame is comprised of three synthetic chemicals—aspartic acid, phenylalanine, and methanol—that have been referred to as chemical poisons.

In 1994, the U.S. Department of Health and Human Services attributed to aspartame over 75 percent of reported adverse food reactions, including headaches, dizziness, seizures, nausea, tachycardia (rapid heart rate), insomnia, numbness, rashes, weight gain, vision problems, hearing loss, breathing difficulties, anxiety, slurred speech, loss of taste, tinnitus (ringing in the ears), vertigo, memory loss, and joint pain. Physicians studying the adverse effects of aspartame found that brain tumors, multiple sclerosis, epilepsy, chronic fatigue syndrome, Parkinson's disease, Alzheimer's disease, mental retardation, lymphoma, birth defects, fibromyalgia, and diabetes could all be triggered or caused by aspartame.

Yeast

The yeast species Saccharomyces Cerevisiae has been used in baking and fermenting alcoholic beverages for thousands of years. It is a single cell fungi.

Other species, such as Candida, are parasitic imperfect fungi that resemble yeast. They are usually harmless. In a healthy body, they are eliminated. However, in an acidic environment they can thrive and cause infection in humans.

My Personal Bout with Candida

Candida is common in people who have taken antibiotics, have a mineral deficiency, eat a lot of refined white sugar and flour, and have large amounts of rancid fat stored in their tissue. Well, that was me. Years ago my body was a good host for this harmful parasite. My symptoms included a craving for sweets, mood swings, allergies, and lack of sexual desire. My skin was dry and I had occasional cold sores and bloating.

When I eliminated this fungal parasite, my symptoms disappeared. I remedied this condition by going on a special regimen for 30 days. I started each day with 2 tablespoons of brewers' yeast (not an active yeast, so it will not promote fungal growth) in a large cup of hot water with ¼ teaspoon RealSalt. I avoided sugar, alcohol, dairy, and salt (except for RealSalt). I also avoided fermented foods such as vinegar, tofu, and soy sauce. I ate up to 4 cups of raw veggies daily, some brown rice, barley, and goat's yogurt as well as 3 cayenne pepper capsules and 3 acidophilus capsules twice a day with meals. I also took herbal extracts such as gotu kola, centaury, Hawthorne leaf, sarsaparilla, and goldenrod for my intestines, liver, kidneys, and lymph system.

I learned that sugar feeds active yeast and that all fermented foods create yeast in the body. The idea is to starve the active yeast parasite by changing the environment in which it thrives.

To get rid of Candida:
- Avoid all sugar, including high sugar content fruits like grapes, pineapples, and bananas.
- Avoid consumption of fermented foods like mushrooms, tofu, beer, wine, and tamari (soy sauce).
- Avoid all breads containing yeast, such as hamburger and hot dog buns and pizza crust.

The next step is to neutralize active yeast with inactive yeast, specifically brewers' yeast.

Once Candida is eliminated, you can reintroduce sugar and fermented foods to your diet in moderation. It is unnecessary to avoid fermented products and foods containing yeast for the rest of your life. Just don't overdo it, and be sure to alkalize with lots of fresh veggies and low-sugar fruits such as raspberries and papayas. A healthy body can properly digest and eliminate sugars and fermentation.

As long as they are the right foods, eating fermented foods in moderation actually helps the body to balance the micro-flora and fauna in the small intestine. Most people agree that tofu is good for you, but it is essential that you use organic tofu because it may be genetically modified and the processing can be toxic.

Keep in mind that cleansing the body of toxins and parasites is needed periodically. Candida's presence often is indicated by increased allergies. For years I suffered with chronic allergy attacks, and now I rarely have allergy symptoms.

Gluten

What is gluten? Gluten is a protein component of whole grains such as wheat, barley, and kamut.

What does it mean to be gluten intolerant? The body is unable to digest gluten often due to a B12 deficiency. B12 is the vitamin that helps our bodies produce protease, which is necessary for the digestion of gluten.

If you find you are having trouble digesting gluten (whole grain breads and pasta), just avoid those foods until you replenish your vitamin B12. Then gradually reintroduce whole grain bread and pasta, and avoid oats and rye. Don't overdo it, but you don't have to avoid gluten for the rest of your life either! Choosing a gluten-free diet is depriving your body of essential nutrients, especially considering that organic whole wheat is the most nutritious grain on earth!

Remember that the B vitamins work synergistically and need to be taken in the B-complex form with potassium from a food source to be assimilated.

Lactose

What is lactose? Lactose is milk sugar, found in milk and milk products.

What does it mean to be lactose intolerant? The body is unable to digest lactose often due to a vitamin B6 deficiency. Vitamin B6 helps our body produce lactase, which is necessary for the digestion of lactose.

While I advise against all cow dairy except organic heavy cream and unsalted butter, if you have trouble digesting cow dairy products, try switching to goat dairy and consider taking a B- complex formula that contains B6 derived from a food source so that your body can assimilate it. As I replenished my B-complex I improved digestion overall. Usually the recommended dosage is too low for someone with a deficiency, but check with your doctor.

Exceptions to my recommendation against cow dairy are organic heavy cream and organic unsalted butter, which are fats that contain CLA. Also colostrum is sometimes used as a dietary supplement for its healing properties and is beneficial to the immune system.

CHAPTER SEVEN

Special Benefits of Super Enzyme Foods

THE BENEFITS OF SUPER ENZYME FOODS EXTEND BEYOND DIGESTION. This chapter addresses some of the other improvements you may see in your health as a result of Living Beyond Organic.

Super Enzyme Foods and Light Frequency

Energy from the sun can be most effective when pure light is separated into its components: gold, yellow, green, blue, violet, orange, and red. Like a prism, water has the power to separate the light from the sun into this seven-color spectrum. Each color is a unique frequency essential to the production of hormones in its corresponding gland.

Thus, the seven hormone-producing glands are essentially the light centers of the body. Each Super Enzyme Food holds a specific light frequency that supports, nourishes, and corresponds to a particular organ in the body. Lacking any one of these colors starts a degeneration process in the body, so the integration of the full spectrum is the key to strengthening and sustaining your life force. Listed below is each color with the corresponding elements that resonate at the same frequency. Exposure to sunlight, plus the intake of water and Super Enzyme Foods, provide the light frequency you need for optimum health.

SUPER ENZYME FOODS AND LIGHT FREQUENCY

COLOR	ORGAN	HERB	FRUIT
GOLD	Pituitary gland	Marigold	Lemon
	Gallbladder	Alfalfa	Raspberry
	Brain	Chamomile	Avocado
	Spleen	Witch hazel	All dark grapes
	Teeth	Lemon balm *(Melissa)*	Red onion
	Sinuses, tonsils	Blue flag	Leek
YELLOW	Pineal gland	Mustard	Apricot
	Inner ear	Suma leaf	Ginger
	Liver	Hawthorne leaf	Crookneck squash
	Bones	Marshmallow	Barley
GREEN	Thyroid	Cayenne *(Capsicum)*	Rosemary
	Eyes, olfactory	Myrrh	Broccoli
	Taste buds	Red beet	Guava
	Spinal cord nerves	Horseradish	Passion fruit
BLUE	Mammary glands	American ginseng	Cilantro
	Heart, lungs	Yerba santa	Mandarin orange
	Lymph	Cranberry	Fig
	Respiratory tract	Goldenrod	Bananas *(after five hours of sunlight)*

COLOR	ORGAN	HERB	FRUIT
VIOLET	Kidneys	Sarsaparilla	Papaya
	Bladder	Kava kava	Tomato
	Skin	White willow bark	Pineapple
	Solar plexus	Passionflower Lemon balm	Hawthorne berry
ORANGE	Pancreas	Thyme	Red kidney beans
	Appendix, colon, white blood cells	Raspberry leaf	Kiwi
	Bile duct	Gotu kola	Red potato
	Small intestine, stomach, pancreatic duct	Centaury	Plum
RED	Testicles, ovaries	Anise seed	Mango
		Noni *(Morinda)*	Wheat
		Juniper berry	Organic corn
		Angelica root *(dong quail)*	Pear

Source: Jonathan: Thunder: Wolf and Morning: Spirit: Wolf: *Doctors of Raphaology Medicine, Universal College of Indigenous Medicine and Natural Arts Healing Center*

The Golden Team

The Golden Team is the group of foods that contains the highest amount of nutrition, light, and life obtainable from a food source. By adding the Golden Team to your life, you will feel tremendous change in your physical and emotional well-being. They are olive oil, sprouted wheat, horseradish, thyme, and red wine (aged seven years or more).

Olives or Extra Virgin Olive Oil

Olives contain the highest quality of oil known. All through history, olive oil has been known as the "oil of kings." It increases the body's ability to transport cholesterol from the arterial walls of the liver where it is broken down into bile salts and used in the formation of bile. The digestion of fats in the gastrointestinal tract is increased tremendously with the help of olive oil. The immune system is strengthened by olive oil's ability to increase production of healthy white blood cells and to bind to and neutralize toxins that attack the body.

Sprouted Wheat

Westerners refer to wheat as the staff of life. It encourages growth and strength, boosts the immune system, neutralizes radiation and toxins, and supplies the body with energy. Extensive research has been conducted on wheat's ability to increase the longevity of the body. Wheat absorbs a wider range of minerals from rich soil than other grains do. Wheat is the most nutritious grain on earth and is an ideal food for human growth and development.

Horseradish

The root is a strong antibacterial agent and is good for reducing mucous congestion and muscle aches and pains. It stimulates blood flow and increases the digestion of bad cholesterol along walls of the blood vessels. Ingesting horseradish is like spring-cleaning your system, helping it to expel bad cholesterol, old mucus, harmful bacteria, yeast infections, and parasites.

Thyme

The herb activates and strengthens the entire body, especially when the organs of the body lack energy. Thyme is one of the strongest antiseptics found in nature, having been used for healing wounds, purifying air, and cleansing the mouth. Common problems such as obesity, physical weakness, emotional instability, and female issues, often caused by hormonal imbalances or weak digestion, can be avoided through the strengthening properties of thyme. Thyme helps to improve all aspects of physical performance and increases efficiency, endurance, and alertness. It is the herb of choice while progressing physically and emotionally toward being whole.

Red Wine

To offer its magical benefits, red wine must be aged at least seven years, during which time a molecular restructuring occurs. Red wine helps the body produce Co Q-10, the co-enzyme that gives the heart its electrical impetus to keep beating. The fanfare about Co Q-10 is rightfully earned, given that its connection to the heart facilitates the brain's ability to release its attachment to emotional trauma. Co Q-10 is also a powerful antioxidant that helps the body convert food into energy, helps neutralize cell damaging free radicals, and has been linked to preventing cancer, heart attacks, and other diseases associated with free radical damage.

I look for red wines such as Bordeaux, Cabernet, Pinot Noir, Merlot, Zinfandel, Rioja, and Chianti.

In addition to the aforementioned benefits, aged red wine helps the body relax and let go of shocks associated with past traumas by releasing the impact of negative feelings, habits, and conditioning. The energetic properties of the wine are enhanced when you drink it with the intention to relax and let go of the aforementioned feelings. To go forward into a future of creativity and excitement, you need to let go of all the negative emotions that bind you to the past and keep you in the mode of self-limiting behavior. Although organic is preferred, it is not essential. We suggest imbibing in moderation. Remember that too much of a good thing is simply too much.

Other Alcohols Included in the
Beyond Organic Lifestyle

Vodka

The only spirit (other than your own) that I recommend is Absolut vodka, because it is not over-processed and is made from wheat grain grown in the fields of Århus, Sweden. What is unique and best is that it is minimally distilled and retains its enzymatic and nutritional properties. It literally is an extract like an essential oil. For more than a hundred years the distillation and rectification process has maintained the highest quality. It contains natural enzymes and pure spring water from its local well.

Beer

I am not a spokesperson for Coors Light. However, at this time it is the only beer we use. Coors Light uses the clear glacial water from the Colorado Rockies to make a special brew with barley and hops that is uniquely frost brewed at an icy 34 degrees. It is aged in glass-lined tanks, and because of its enzymatic properties, it has an expiration date. It is always refrigerated to maintain freshness.

Sake (unfiltered preferred)

Sake is made from brown rice grain, koji enzymes, sake yeast, and water. Using a process called multiple parallel fermentation, koji (a type of mold) converts rice starch to sugar, and yeast converts sugar to alcohol. Nigori (cloudy), daiginjo-junmai (no added alcohol during fermentation with 50 percent polished rice), and other unfiltered varieties are unpasteurized and unfiltered, and they contain no artificial additives, enhancers, or sulfites. They don't require aging and are ready to drink when bottled. Sake is low in alcohol content and calories compared with distilled spirits. It contains trace minerals such as calcium, iron, potassium, and magnesium. Nigori sake is preferred because it uses more of the whole rice grain. As with all whole foods, each component part helps every other part to be digested.

In the practice of Raphaology the above alcohols are used in moderation when needed to release trapped emotional, physical, and mental stress and trauma.

Alcohol therapies are unique to the practice of Raphaology. Specialized dosages are determined by a Raphaology practitioner for the purpose of clearing energetic blocks.

| YAMS for
HORMONAL BALANCE |

As someone once said
to me, "If it tastes good
and is good for me, of course
I would switch. I'm not crazy!"

CHAPTER EIGHT

Make the Switch from MAD to Super

MAD IS AN ACRONYM FOR THE MODERN AMERICAN DIET. I WAS ignorant about good nutrition for the first 40 years of my life, buying over-processed, enriched foods and eating acid-producing fruits and vegetables. I changed, and you can too!

This list was designed to make the switch easier for you. When a recipe calls for a MAD choice, you have a quick reference to the Super Alternative.

VEGETABLES

MAD Choice	Super Alternative
Bell peppers *(red, green yellow)*	Anaheim chilies
Bok choy	Swiss chard
Cabbage	Kale, radicchio, Swiss chard
Carrots	Garnet yams
Celery	Fennel, anise bulb
Garlic	Elephant garlic
Green onions, scallions	Chive, leeks
Iceberg lettuce	Butter lettuce
Mature Romaine or red leaf lettuce mix	Belgian endive, baby lettuce mix

VEGETABLES *(continued)*

MAD Choice	Super Alternative
Mushrooms *(button, white, straw)*	Mushroom *(crimini, shiitake, chanterelle)*
Onions *(white, yellow)*	Red onions
Potatoes *(russet, white)*	Red potatoes
Pumpkins	Garnet yams
Radishes	Jicama
Turnips	Beets
Zucchini, other squashes	Crookneck squash

GRAINS, BEANS, AND LEGUMES

MAD Choice	Super Alternative
Beans *(pinto, black)*	Anasazi or dark red kidney beans
Garbanzos	Soy or white beans
Green peas	Edamame, baby lima beans
Flour *(bleached, enriched pastry)*	Organic whole wheat or barley flour
Lentils *(green, yellow)*	Red lentils
Oatmeal	Rolled barley
Rice *(white, jasmine)*	Brown rice, brown basmati, or wild rice

FRUITS

MAD Choice	Super Alternative
Apples	Pears
Blueberries	Bilberries, blackberries, boysenberries
Goji berries	Organic red raisins, dried cranberries, red currants, concord grapes, dark cherries

FRUITS *(continued)*

MAD Choice	Super Alternative
Grapes *(green, white)*	Dark grapes *(red, blue, purple, black)*
Oranges, grapefruit	Tangerines, mandarin oranges
Tomatoes	Tomatoes *(Roma/plum, heirloom)*
Watermelon	Cantaloupe or honeydew melon

NUTS, SEEDS, AND NUT BUTTERS

MAD Choice	Super Alternative
Macadamia nuts	Brazil nuts
Peanut butter	Almond or cashew butter
Peanuts	Cashews
Pistachio nuts	Almonds
Pumpkin seeds	Sunflower seeds
Walnuts	Pine nuts

DAIRY AND EGGS

MAD Choice	Super Alternative
Buttermilk	Goat's yogurt
Cheese *(cow's milk)*	Goat's or sheep's milk cheese
Chicken eggs	Duck eggs
Creamers *(flavored, half-and-half, etc.)*	Organic heavy whipping cream, fresh almond milk
Margarine, butter	Organic unsalted butter, coconut butter
Shortening, lard	Organic unsalted butter, coconut butter

make the switch from MAD to Super

MEAT, FISH, AND SEAFOOD

MAD Choice	Super Alternative
Beef, veal, pork, lamb	Bison
Chicken	Organic extra firm tofu
Crab, scallops, lobster	Jumbo shrimp *(freshwater or ocean)*
Halibut, tuna, cod, shark	Orange roughy, lake trout, wild salmon
Turkey	Bison roast

SPECIALTY FOODS

MAD Choice	Super Alternative
Commercial ice cream	Coconut, rice, soy, and goat's milk ice cream
Cornstarch	Organic cornstarch
Enriched cream-filled cookies	Organic cookies made with evaporated cane juice, nonhydrogenated fat, whole wheat *(Health Valley Cookie Creams)*
Enriched graham crackers	Whole wheat graham crackers *(New Morning, Go Go Grahams)*
Enriched wheat flakes	Whole grain flakes *(Weetabix, Kashi)*
Frozen juice blend bars	100% fruit juice bars
Milk chocolate	Organic dark chocolate
Milk chocolate chips	Organic dark chocolate chips
Milk chocolate syrup	Organic chocolate syrup
Prepared tomato paste	Rehydrated sun-dried Roma tomatoes*
Pretzels	Whole wheat sesame sticks
White bread	Whole grain bread *(sprouted barley, wheat berry)*
White flat bread	Whole wheat lavash

* Combine 12 sun-dried tomato halves and 1 cup boiling pure water. Cover and steep for 20 minutes. Add seasoning (RealSalt, cayenne, herbs) to taste; blend until smooth (30 seconds to 1 minute).

BEVERAGES

MAD Choice	Super Alternative
Acai berry juice	Noni juice
Aloe vera juice	Thyme/chamomile tea, potato water extract*
Apple juice	Coconut water or pear juice
Beer	Cold brew process made with barley and hops *(Coors Light)*
Black tea	Juniper berry tea
Champagne	Sparkling unfiltered sake
Chocolate milk	Goat's milk and organic chocolate syrup
Coffee	Papua New Guinea Coffee
Colas	Organic root beer
Fruit punch	Cranberry and concord grape blend
Ginger ale	Ginger beer
Grape soda	Concord grape juice, natural sparkling mineral water
Hot cocoa	Organic cocoa powder and Sucanat
Italian soda	Pure fruit juice, simple syrup, organic heavy cream, natural sparkling mineral water
Lemon/lime soft drinks	Lemon or lime juice, simple syrup or raw honey, and natural sparkling mineral water
Milkshake	Fruit smoothie or milk shake made with goat's milk
Orange juice	Tangerine juice, pineapple juice
Over-processed vodka	Minimally processed vodka *(Absolut)*
Red wine	Red wine *(aged seven years or longer)*
Soda water	Natural sparkling mineral water *(San Pellegrino)*

* *See recipe on page 25.*

make the switch from MAD to Super

BEVERAGES *(continued)*

MAD Choice	Super Alternative
White wine	Dry sake

Note that over-consumption of alcoholic beverages can cause high blood sugar levels, dehydration, and premature aging. Be sure to drink water to neutralize these negative side effects. You need about two glasses of water for every drink containing alcohol to neutralize the dehydration effects.

HERBS, SPICES, AND CONDIMENTS

MAD Choice	Super Alternative
Curry powder	Organic curry powder*
Ketchup	Zesty Catch-Up *(see recipe on page 216)*
Sour cream	Pure sour cream or crème fraîche or goat's yogurt
Parsley	Cilantro
Pepper *(black or white)*	Cayenne pepper
Salt *(iodized or regular sea salt)*	RealSalt
Soy sauce	Organic low sodium tamari, Super Ponzu *(see recipe on page 204)*
Sandwich spread	Antioxidant Sandwich Spread *(see recipe on page 128)*
Tartar sauce	Super Tartar Sauce *(see recipe on page 204)*
Artificial vanilla flavoring	Organic vanilla extract
Vinegar *(white, apple cider)*	Red wine, brown rice, balsamic, plum vinegar

OILS

MAD Choice	Super Alternative
Canola oil	Safflower oil, sunflower oil

* with no black pepper

OILS *(continued)*

MAD Choice	Super Alternative
Macadamia nut oil	Coconut oil
Generic vegetable oil	Safflower oil, sunflower oil, organic corn oil, cold pressed extra virgin olive oil
Peanut oil	Sesame oil

SWEETENERS

MAD Choice	Super Alternative
Artificial sweeteners	Stevia, blackstrap molasses
High fructose corn syrup	Simple Syrup (*see recipe on page 197*) or 100% vegetable glycerin
Honey (Grade A)	Raw, wild honey, brown rice syrup
Maple syrup (Grade A) or maple-flavored syrup	Grade B maple syrup
Powdered sugar	Blended fructose and organic corn starch
Sugar *(refined white, brown)*	Dehydrated or evaporated cane juice *(Sucanat)*, unrefined crystalline fructose

"Obtaining the nutrients you need to stay healthy without eating meat or animal fat is impossible. Like the vegetarian diet, the raw food diet is notoriously lacking in quality protein, minerals, vitamins, (most notably vitamins A, D, and B12), and essential fatty acids."

— JORDAN S. RUBIN, N.M.D.
AND JOSEPH BRASCO, M.D.

ASPARAGUS for
| MEGA NUTRIENTS |

*A high functioning
digestive system is necessary
to absorb 100% of the
nutrients in whole wheat.*

CHAPTER NINE

Vegetarian Diets and Super Enzyme Foods

I WAS A VEGETARIAN FOR A TIME. BUT I FOUND THAT THE LIFESTYLE that works for me offers a complete spectrum of nutrients found in particular meat, fish, eggs, dairy products, fruits, vegetables, nuts, and seeds.

We will use the following definitions in discussing vegetarian lifestyles:

- **Raw Foodists**—eat all their food in its raw state, including meat, eggs, and dairy. Except for wild-caught salmon and grass-fed bison, the risks of eating raw meat far outweigh the benefits. Also, when par cooked, certain vegetables' toxins are destroyed, and their nutrients are better absorbed and more beneficial to the digestive tract.

- **Vegans**—eat fruit, vegetables, leafy greens, nuts, seeds, grains, and legumes, but abstain from meat, dairy, eggs, and honey. Although this lifestyle can be high in digestive enzymes, it is restrictive and lacks certain essential fatty acids and amino acids.

- **Lacto-vegetarians**—do not eat meat, but they do eat dairy.

- **Vegetarians**—eat fruits, vegetables, and occasionally dairy and eggs but not meat, fish, or poultry.

My life experience and research have led me to believe that most vegetarian diets are lacking in nutrients that can be found only in certain animal products. However, if your choice is to exclude animal products, I suggest that organic whole wheat be a daily staple. It is the single most nutritious grain on earth and requires a fully functioning digestive system to absorb and assimilate it. If you do have trouble digesting it, try switching to brown rice or barley for a week while adding a B-complex supplement. Gradually introduce wheat by combining it with brown rice or barley for another week before eating 100 percent wheat products.

I have found that strict vegetarian lifestyles work well for cleansing and rejuvenating the body on a short-term basis, 21 days or less. However, long-term vegetarianism can have adverse side effects such as weakness, headaches, fatigue, foggy thinking, anemia, and reduced resistance to infection.

I am comfortable with the following lifestyle:

- **First**: Focus on eating Super Enzyme Foods, which include specific meats, fish, eggs, and dairy in addition to fruits, vegetables, nuts, and seeds.

- **Second**: Plan vegetarian days once or twice a week, especially after eating meats, after parties, and during the holidays. This gives your body a chance to recover by allowing your enzymes to focus on repair work instead of digestion.

- **Third**: Incorporate a purely raw food diet one to three days per month for cleansing so toxins don't get a chance to build up. Raw food has a very alkalizing effect and helps you eliminate toxins. I also like to include:

  - **Beyond Lemon Cleanse**—made with 8 ounces natural spring water, 1 fresh lemon juiced, 1 tablespoon Grade B or C maple syrup, a dash to ¼ teaspoon cayenne pepper, and 15 drops to 1 teaspoon B-complex with potassium as needed. This combination of ingredients is antibacterial, improves circulation, neutralizes acidity, replenishes minerals, and helps to clear out toxins.

  - **INS wheatgrass powder**—rich source of chlorophyll, vitamins, minerals, and enzymes like SOD (Super Oxide Dismutase), excellent for neutralizing and clearing out toxins, reduces inflammation and inhibits the metabolic activity of carcinogens. As part of our daily regimen we combine one sachet of wheatgrass powder in a glass of water with B-complex at least once a day to boost our immune system. (In rare cases it may cause detoxification symptoms like rash, hives, headache, and diarrhea.) In the event that this reaction occurs, it may be that the healing properties of the wheatgrass are stimulating the release of stored toxins.

What Everyone, Vegetarian or Not, Needs to Know: Complete Proteins

Nine essential amino acids are required to form a complete protein. While some foods are complete proteins in and of themselves, by combining foods that provide these nine essential amino acids you can create a complete protein. Complete protein combinations are easiest for your body to digest to provide protein nutrients where needed. The following are suggestions for complete protein combinations:

- Brown rice, red kidney beans, and organic corn
- Barley and red lentils
- Anasazi beans and brown rice pasta
- Buckwheat and yams
- Red potato and goat's or sheep's milk feta cheese
- Organic Edamame and whole wheat pasta
- Whole wheat and navy beans or kidney beans or lima beans
- Bulgur, red onions or leeks, and avocados (tabouli)

The following are good complete protein sources: raw almonds; raw cashews; water buffalo milk, cheese, or yogurt; goat's milk, cheese, or yogurt; sheep's milk, cheese, or yogurt; duck eggs; organic tofu; and, of course, bison. By the way, many of my vegetarian friends have tried and enjoyed bison without any ill effects.

ELEPHANT GARLIC
| IMPROVES CIRCULATION |

*The goal is to find
balance between
information and
practical application.*

C H A P T E R   T E N

The Beyond Organic Kitchen

PLEASE READ THE INFORMATION IN THIS SECTION BEFORE ATTEMPTing to cook your Super Enzyme Foods.

Simply avoid aluminum and nonstick cookware items altogether.

Sponsored research would like you to believe ingesting minute amounts of aluminum is not harmful, but daily and over a lifetime? Or that so long as you don't cook with temperatures above 500 degrees F., the Teflon/non-stick coating does not release PFOA (perfluorooctanoic) and other toxic gasses. But DuPont's own scientists have concluded that polymer fume fever in humans is possible at 662°F., a temperature easily exceeded when a pan is preheated on a burner or placed beneath a broiler, or in a self-cleaning oven.

In addition pans can become scratched or chipped, and the synthetic particles can contaminate your food. Even when they are not chipped, chemicals of the coating can contaminate your food when exposed to high temperatures, triggering the release of toxic gasses. Instead, I recommend that you invest in a set of stainless- steel pots and pans, heavy gauge with tight-fitting lids. Also cooking with cast iron, copper, glass, or porcelain are great choices that are safe for cooking and enhance the Beyond Organic Kitchen.

Beyond Organic Kitchen Checklist

- Use only pots, pans, bakeware, and skillets that are stainless steel, cast iron, glass, porcelain, or copper.
- Make certain all cooking utensils are stainless steel.
- Bake cookies and pizza on a baking stone or on stainless-steel baking pans.
- Use a glass cutting board for food preparation.
- Use bottled water for all recipes, coffee, tea, etc.
- Store food in glass containers with airtight lids; do not store in plastic.
- Refrigerate leftover food within 2 hours to prevent harmful bacteria growth.
- Use leftover cooked food within 48 to 72 hours.
- Refrigerate all open bottles of oil (especially olive oil).
- Use high-smoke-point oils like safflower for cooking (refer to Super Enzyme Foods list).
- Replace plastic food storage bags with unbleached wax paper bags.
- Wash all fresh produce in clean water with 1 drop of food-grade hydrogen peroxide for approximately 15 seconds.

What to Avoid in Your Meal Preparation and Food Storage

- Microwave use of *any* kind (defrosting food, heating water for tea or coffee, reheating food, popcorn, etc.)
- Cooking in aluminum foil and using aluminum cookware and utensils
- Cooking on synthetic nonstick surfaces
- Cutting boards and utensils made of porous material such as wood, plastic, or rubber
- Plastic storage containers (breed bacteria)

- Plastic food storage bags (can release harmful gasses at warm temperatures and contaminate food)
- Direct contact between food and plastic wrap or aluminum foil (try using a protective layer of parchment paper or unbleached waxed paper bags) when storing
- Cooking in olive oil (it is highly enzymatic and fragile and must be used in its raw state)
- Storing olive oil at room temperature for more than 2 weeks

Cancer in the Kitchen: Microwave Ovens

I was never comfortable using a microwave oven. I always felt that I should wear a lead vest or run out of the room after pressing the start button, but I eventually gave in to using it for convenience. I used it for reheating food, defrosting food before cooking, baking potatoes, and heating frozen meals. I was sensitive to the change in texture and taste of the food once it was nuked. Food was always too hot in the center. I remember being extra careful and blowing on each bite before feeding my daughter. Many of my friends had the same reservations about using a microwave at first, but it soon became routine, and even though we did not cook our meals in the microwave, we did reheat our food in it. There are a few things you need to know about microwaves to make an informed decision about them.

Microwaves are short waves of alternating currents of electromagnetic energy that heat by friction. This friction causes the food cell nucleus to implode, which is why the food is always burning hot in the middle. This mutated molecule is now a harmful free radical carcinogen (cancer-causing agent).

This cellular degeneration has been proven through scientific study. Clinical trials performed in Switzerland by Dr. Hans Ulrich Hertel show the destructive force microwaves have on a food molecule. In this experiment, a test group was administered three categories of foods: raw, conventionally heated, and microwaved. The study confirmed that after two months, all volunteers who ate raw and conventionally heated food had no problems. Those who ate microwaved foods showed blood damage. Dr. Hertel found that "because of the force involved, the cells are actually broken, the very life of the cells impaired, making them easy prey for viruses, fungi, and other microorganisms."

The effects on blood cells vary depending on the individual. For example, high levels of vitamins A and E could help scavenge the free radicals, which could have an effect on the white blood cells necessary to fight the invasion.

Repeated ingestion of microwaved foods overwhelms the body's immunological factors at an alarming rate. Cumulative totals of microwave toxins are a direct cause of cellular mutation, organ dysfunction, tissue damage, nerve degeneration, and immune failure. Ask yourself how you can continue using a microwave when the effects are:

- Interference with and hindrance of normal digestive processes
- Deterioration of nerve impulses
- Constriction and blockage of lymphatic fluids
- Interruption of normal hormone production
- Interrupted sleep
- Loss of memory and ability to concentrate

Every time you "nuke" nutritionally rich, life-infusing foods, you are left with a toxic, dis-ease promoting, and carcinogen-riddled mass of mutated particles. Is it worth the convenience?

About Household Products

We are bombarded with toxins and airborne contaminants each and every day. Every time we drive our cars or walk near the busy streets, we inhale toxic emissions from cars, buses, and leaf blowers. In our homes, we breathe fumes from pesticides, disinfectants, and air fresheners that contain chemicals. We moisturize our skin with synthetic humectants in our cosmetics and wash our clothes in laundry detergent made with petrochemicals. We need to take inventory of this and start paying attention. These toxins and contaminants affect our health. Read the labels on the products in your home. Use of products with ingredients that include ammonia, acetone, alcohol, formalin, propylene glycol, and petroleum-based products, especially in the spray form, increases the risk of asthma.

There are natural, less toxic alternatives to these products:

- Use a solution of water and white vinegar instead of ammonia-based window cleaner.
- Use biodegradable dishwasher soap.
- Use biodegradable laundry soap.
- Use natural citrus-based air freshener.
- Use an olive oil-based moisturizer instead of a petroleum-based one.
- Use a mild solution of dishwashing liquid and water as insecticide for plants.
- Use water-based paint instead of a heavy metal-based one.
- Use ½ cup white vinegar or baking soda instead of toxic bleach.

Once you eliminate use of these harsh chemicals in your home and on your clothes, you will notice that common health disorders like coughing, wheezing, nasal congestion, burning eyes, headache, burning skin, rashes, muscle aches, irritability, mental confusion, and hyperactivity will diminish. You may even notice your sense of smell will improve.

The next step, in addition to keeping your home environment free of toxic chemicals, is to keep live plants which can help to clean, purify, and oxygenate the air we breathe. I find the Peace Lily (spathiphyllum) is easy to care for and also helps absorb chemicals like alcohol, acetone, trichloroethylene, benzene, and formaldehyde that might be lingering in the air. And I always keep fresh thyme plants by my electronic devices (especially in front of computer monitors and televisions) to help absorb emissions. The beneficial effects of plants go beyond the physical and include psychological benefits as well. Research shows that keeping plants in your living and work space may lead to an increase in positive feelings, and a reduction in feelings of anxiety. Initially the plants will need to be replaced more often as the absorption of toxic emissions from chemicals, computers, televisions, and cell phones will deplete the plants. As you detoxify the environment the plants will last longer. NASA researcher Dr. Wolverton suggests one plant per 100 square feet of living space. For more information: *www.wolvertonenvironmental.com*

Does Stress Affect Your Health?

Stress alone can be the number one cause of dis-ease. Stanford University, one of the top biomedical research centers in the country, has found that chronically activated stress can cause damage and accelerate disease. The researchers linked stress to cardiovascular disease, weakened immunity, and nerve and brain dysfunction. I know I have experienced stress-related headaches, backaches, muscle spasms, diarrhea, stomach acid, chest pains, and more. When in addition to stress we increase our acid production by eating indigestible food, we create an acidic environment in which bacteria thrive. At that point, it is a miracle that we are functioning at all.

Daily cardiovascular exercise helps your body to produce and release endorphins (the feel-good hormones) that reduce stress. The following information is a good guide for those who need to exercise but don't have a regular exercise regimen established.

Importance of Exercise

"Exercise is one of the best ways to increase your HDL (good cholesterol) level."

—DR. DONALD PLANCE, OSTEOPATHIC PHYSICIAN

I have a few tips that will help to increase circulation and oxygenation in your body and maximize the benefits of walking for your daily exercise:

Stretch before you begin

- Raise your arms above your head; reach with the right hand, then the left; alternate reaching and pulling down as if you were climbing a rope.
- Stand with your feet shoulder width apart and your hands on your hips to keep your balance; do four slow neck rolls to the right; then repeat to the left.

- Raise your shoulders up to your ears and down again. Repeat four times.
- Do shoulder rolls forward and backward four times each.

While walking

- Remember to breathe. Take long deep breaths, hold four seconds, and exhale slowly.
- Take nice long strides.
- Walk at a brisk pace.
- As you walk raise your arms in front of you, then overhead, then reach out to the sides.
- Repeat ten times in concert with your breathing.

If you are not in the habit of exercising regularly, start with 10-minute sessions and add 5-minute increments until you reach 30 minutes. It doesn't matter how long it takes you to build up to it; *the plan* is to:

- Make it a priority.
- Stay consistent.
- Do it every day.

As you stretch, walk, reach, and breathe, visualize your circulation improving. Circulation helps to keep your bones strong, flexible, and dense.

- Visualize oxygen going to all parts of your body, especially your brain.
- Know you are strengthening your body and improving organ function.
- Acknowledge that you are taking time out just for you!

Why is it important to exercise every day?

Because consistent exercise helps:

- Produce and release endorphins that make you feel good about yourself

- Balance hormone production
- Stimulate production of digestive bile for better digestion
- Increase circulation to promote release of built-up toxins
- Increase muscle and skin tone
- Increase HDL (good cholesterol)

Because **FOOD** is only the beginning

Beyond Organic Lifestyle Pyramid

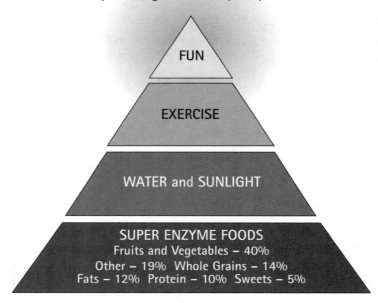

FUN

EXERCISE

WATER and SUNLIGHT

SUPER ENZYME FOODS
Fruits and Vegetables – 40%
Other – 19%   Whole Grains – 14%
Fats – 12%   Protein – 10%   Sweets – 5%

Beyond Organic Lifestyle Highlights and Suggestions

You sabotage your health both subtly and severely. When damage is sufficient to cause dis-ease, you're likely to do something about it. When it is incremental, you either don't notice or you put the blame on factors out of your control. Regardless of how the damage was sustained, when it is occurring it can be prevented. To ignore this is self-sabotage.

10 Things that Can Sabotage Your Health

Using synthetic drugs

Anything synthetic damages our mineral-based organs, especially the liver, kidneys, and pancreas; however, certain conditions such as old age and advanced medical problems may require use of prescription drugs. Always consult with your healthcare practitioner.

Smoking cigarettes

Smoke deprives oxygen delivery to red blood cells and tissues, causing premature aging. Smoking increases your risk of major dis-eases such as stroke, heart disease, and lung cancer.

Drinking toxic alcohol

Toxic alcohol can cause scar tissue on the liver and mutations in red blood cells, raise sugar levels, and cause acidity and dehydration.

Drinking colas, refined sodas, and sports drinks

Colas and refined sodas inhibit your body's ability to detoxify, and they lower hormone levels, creating an imbalance that can contribute to sexual dysfunction. Sports drinks made with high fructose corn syrup do not hydrate on a cellular level. Only water can do that.

Consuming iodized table salt and common sea salt

These salts destabilize electrolytes (sodium, potassium, magnesium, chloride, phosphate, and bicarbonate), which can cause kidney dysfunction and high blood pressure.

Using bad fats and refined or bleached flour, rice, sugar, and artificial sweeteners

Consuming these items causes acute malnutrition, blood vessel constriction, and heart disease, and can lead to brain damage.

Bathing in and/or drinking chlorinated and fluoridated tap water

This exposure may cause kidney damage and expedite premature aging of the skin.

Engaging in stressful situations

Stress constricts all blood vessels, digestive ducts, and valves, and it raises blood pressure and causes acidity.

Cooking with a microwave oven

Microwave ovens create harmful free radicals that mutate your food on a cellular level and destroy nutrients. When ingested, microwaved food creates acidity and weakens immunity while increasing the risk of developing carcinogenic conditions.

Using aluminum or nonstick cookware

This may lead to heavy-metal poisoning, nerve damage, memory loss, and immune deficiency.

10 Great Things You Can Do for Your Health

Eat Super Enzyme Foods, organic if available.

They are alkalizing and help you balance your pH, which deters bacterial growth. By preventing the development of virus and fungus, we build a strong immune system. Particularly when consumed in their raw state, Super Enzyme Foods' enzyme content ensures nutrient absorption, thereby preventing and removing toxic buildup.

Eat 60 percent raw food at each meal.

This provides your body with exogenous enzymes needed for proper organ function, including digestion and cell renewal. If raw food is not available, use vegetarian digestive enzyme supplements as needed.

Drink a minimum of 64 ounces (eight 8-ounce glasses)
of natural spring water daily.

Hydrate your cells and deter the aging process. We have 4½ gallons of fluid (lymphatic, cellular, and blood) in our body, which needs to be replaced every nine days. Try adding 2 to 3 drops of natural mint-flavored liquid chlorophyll from alfalfa to an

8-ounce glass of water. It is refreshing and oxygenating and makes it easier to adjust to drinking more water.

Get a minimum of 4 to 8 hours of uninterrupted sleep per night.

Sleep is necessary for organ repair and electrolyte balance. Initially, more sleep is needed during detoxification. Less sleep is required for a fully functioning healthy body.

Exercise 30 minutes daily.

Walking, using a trampoline, biking, or swimming is best. These activities are low impact and gentle on the joints. They stimulate circulation, release trapped toxins, and increase muscle and skin tone by allowing amino acids to strengthen connective tissues that hold cells in place and keep mutated cells from spreading.

Get 20 minutes of morning sun each day.

This is a super immune booster. It increases vitamin D production and stabilizes all hormone production by allowing your body to synthesize vitamin D from the sun's ultraviolet rays. Protect your skin with olive oil; avoid synthetic sunscreen products that cause distortion. Apply zinc topically when exposure to sun is prolonged. When you buy sun block, look for natural ingredients. Your skin absorbs what you put on it. If you can't eat it, don't put it on your skin.

Use skincare and cosmetics free of chemicals and artificial preservatives.

Use makeup, fragrance, skin and hair care products made with natural ingredients.

When exposed to toxins, your skin can become clogged with chemicals which produce toxicity and can lead to abnormal skin growths.

Feminine Hygiene Products

Use of organic cotton products reduces your risk of toxic shock syndrome and other complications that can result from products that contain chemicals for absorbency and synthetic deodorants.

I use Natracare. It is the only company I have found that makes 100 percent organic cotton tampons. It is critical that we understand how important this is to our health. Remember: Our bodies can absorb toxins through the skin, so it doesn't make sense that we knowingly insert a potentially harmful substance into our body and then keep it there for hours at a time!

Breathe deeply to oxygenate the blood and clear your mind.

Slowly inhale deeply into the diaphragm (not into the chest) for four counts. Hold your breath for four counts, and then exhale slowly for four counts. Pause for four counts. Repeat this process for up to 5 minutes. This will help oxygenate your blood and clear the cobwebs out of your mind. By focusing on your breathing, you can calm and center yourself. This is a great way to begin meditation and counteract shallow breathing. Oxygenating the blood helps to relieve stress and lowers blood pressure. Delivering more oxygen to the detoxifying cells converts nutrients to energy and helps eliminate anaerobic microbes.

Reduce stress by doing something you enjoy each day.

This increases production of endorphins like dopamine, the feel-good hormone. Relax and have fun as often as possible. This will help you learn to love and appreciate yourself and others. We need to create balance in all aspects of our life: physical, mental, and emotional. According to Hiromi Shinya, M.D.: "My research indicates that a surge of positive emotional energy, such as that arising from love, laughter, and joy, can stimulate our DNA to produce a cascade of our body's source enzyme, the miracle enzyme that acts as a bio-catalyst for repairing our cells."

A Beyond Organic Morning

Before you get out of bed, take a deep breath and stretch.

Take a moment to connect with your body. Apply the law of attraction and make an affirmation. Think positive.

Then, *carpe diem* (seize the day)!

Gargle with RealSalt and spring water before breakfast. If your tonsils have been doing their job, you may have accumulated toxins/mucous during the night. It is best to rinse them out. Otherwise, these toxins have to travel through your whole digestive system and may get stored along the way.

First thing in the morning is a great time to introduce fresh fruit into your body to give you an enzymatic infusion. One cup of fresh papaya is perfect. My favorite is Hawaiian, but Mexican and Brazilian varieties are good too. Try them all and discover your favorite. I also enjoy an assortment of berries (raspberries, blackberries, strawberries) on sprouted barley toast with soft goat's cheese and raw wild honey or organic brown rice syrup. Hot brown rice cereal with cream or goat's milk and Sucanat is a great option. A cup of Papua New Guinea Coffee (*see recipe on page 180*) helps clear the colon; regular bowel movements are a sign of good health.

It is best to wash after every bowel movement. Toto washlet is an easily adaptable toilet seat attachment. Also install filters to reduce contaminants such as chlorine and fluoride in the shower.

- Use natural deodorant like Crystal body rock; avoid antiperspirants.
- Use liquid soap or shower gel (avoid soap bars).
- Use natural bristle tooth and hairbrush.
- Wear comfortable natural fabrics (cotton, silk, hemp, wool, bamboo, and linen).

A Beyond Organic Evening

It is important to allow time to unwind and let go of daily stress.

- Eat dinner early—before 6 p.m. is best—so that you have time to digest and absorb nutrients.
- Try a walk after dinner. This promotes good digestion, improves circulation, burns excess calories, and gets you to turn off the TV.
- Engage in fun activities with your partner, spouse, children, parents, friends, and pets too! I know that when we take time out to play Boggle, Scrabble, Clue, or card games, we end up enjoying each other's company and laughing hysterically. Laughter is an excellent way to release stress and produce endorphins.

- Listen to your favorite music; it can inspire you to dance, stretch, meditate, or simply relax.
- Enjoy a Living Beyond Organic Body salt bath (¼ to ½ cup per bath) to help the body hydrate, re-mineralize, release toxins, de-stress, and relax.
- Apply Lavender essential oil to temples, neck, and shoulders at bedtime or during meditation.
- Drink a cup of organic chamomile tea to relax or peppermint tea to stimulate circulation and aid in digestion when needed.
- Apply Living Beyond Organic Body Oil after bath or shower to maintain a youthful glow and protect from exposure to toxic chemicals lurking in your dry cleaning, laundry soap, chlorinated pool, and the environment.
- Before bedtime, always brush teeth and scrub tongue with a natural bristle toothbrush even if you are sleepy. The cleaner your mouth is at bedtime the less bacteria build-up you will have in the morning.
- Use toothpaste free of sodium laurel sulfate and fluoride.
- Use spring water for rinsing your mouth (not tap water).
- Once a week soak your toothbrush in water with a few drops of food-grade hydrogen peroxide. This kills germs.
- Take off your makeup. It traps toxins in the skin and promotes bacterial growth that leads to pimples and blackheads.
- Read a book that interests you, something inspiring or funny.
- Avoid watching news programming, which is usually filled with subject matter and images that are not conducive to a peaceful night's sleep.
- Avoid films that are depressing or violent or contain destructive visual images; they activate your brain and do not promote rest.
- Avoid eating at bedtime. Often, restless sleep or nightmares are related to poor digestion. Allow 2 hours minimum after eating before going to sleep.
- Avoid falling asleep in front of the television. This causes melatonin (sleep hormone) deprivation. Also, the emissions distort your body's electromagnetic field, robbing you of precious

energy you need during sleep to repair damage and restore proper organ function.

- Avoid computer work at bedtime, especially in bed, as it strains your eyes and bathes your body in toxic emissions.

It is best to avoid having a television or computer in the bedroom altogether. The goal at bedtime is to shut down the brain and give it a rest. Tomorrow is another day that will bring plenty of opportunities to activate and use your mind.

As you settle into bed, take a deep breath, exhale slowly, let go of the clutter in your mind, and focus on a positive thought. Close your eyes and remember that this is your body's chance to rest, repair, and rejuvenate.

| SWEET dreams. |

All the information in this book was presented with the intent to share what I have learned on my path toward health with the hope to guide you as I have guided my family and friends. I acknowledge that everyone has a different set of challenges, making it difficult to complete a total lifestyle change. I understand that and want you to know that consistently changing what you can will make a difference. Your results will be directly proportionate to the level of your commitment to this lifestyle.

PAPUA NEW GUINEA COFFEE
| to ELIMINATE TOXINS |

Imagine an extravaganza
of flavor without the
foods that are out of favor.

CHAPTER ELEVEN

21-Day Beyond Organic Menu Plan

Relish a **HEARTY** breakfast.
ENJOY your main course for lunch.
Savor a light **ENZYMATIC** dinner.

MAKING THE SWITCH TO SUPER ENZYME FOODS MAY SEEM CHAL-lenging. After all, if you're like me, you have a longstanding familiarity with your favorite recipes. Because I know how im-portant and necessary to your health making the switch is and how time-consuming it can appear, I've developed a 21-Day Living Beyond Organic Menu Plan, complete with recipes. There is something for everyone in the choices provided.

We are programmed to rush in the morning, giving little or no priority to a nutritious meal. We eat lunch on the run and then try to make up for it at dinner, loading up on extra portions. This is a habit you will have to change!

Cooking not your thing? Have you tried a number of diets and failed? Don't worry! Here you will find simple recipes, menus, and food combinations to get you started. Remember that this is not a diet; rather, you will be Living Beyond Organic with the broad purpose of maximizing your health.

The following menu was written as a transition from the MAD routine of eating your main meal for dinner. Gradually work toward the goal of having a light meal for dinner. Use the following suggestions on a daily basis:

- Have lots of fruit at breakfast.
- Have your main meal at lunch to allow your body time to use the nutrients.
- Have a light dinner, preferably early.

You will find menu suggestions for your first 21 days, followed by recipes. After the first 21 days, you will feel better, realize it's easier than you thought, and be well on your way to customizing your menu to suit your taste and preferences.

All the ingredients in my recipes are rich in enzymes and essential fatty acids that boost and maintain function of organs and glands. Fully functional glands produce hormones that are the fuel for organ function. In addition, specific herbs should be taken to repair existing damage and restore organ and glandular function, as should supplemental vitamins and minerals to replenish vital nutrients.

Mix and match meals as you like. These are only suggested meal plans. Each suggested meal is complete, providing enzymes, protein, carbohydrates, fats, vitamins, and minerals. Keep in mind that organic produce and products are preferred. However, conventional is OK as long as the ingredients are washed thoroughly. **Some exceptions include salmon. Always look for** *wild caught;* **avoid farm raised altogether. Also, always use organic tofu and organic edamame.**

The following tips will enhance the enzymatic benefits of Super Enzyme Foods:

- If weight loss is your intention, drink a glass of water 30 minutes before a meal. In this way, you will be satisfied with smaller portions.
- Don't overeat, or nutrients will go to waste. Whatever your body can't use or eliminate, it will store in fatty tissue.
- Increase your raw food intake.

- Use vegetarian digestive enzyme supplements on cooked food as needed.
- Chew each bite of your food 15 to 30 times. Foods like nuts, meat, and salads require more chewing, while ripe soft foods like avocadoes, pears, and berries require less.
- Eat your fruit between 6 a.m. and noon to convert blood sugar into energy and metabolize vitamins. This recommendation is based on a study at Stanford University School of Medicine.
- Eat salad or raw veggies before a cooked meal. This helps with portion control of cooked foods and will expedite your weight loss and help with weight maintenance.
- Drink fresh vegetable blends for an enzymatic energy boost in the afternoon.
- Adjusting to drinking more water? Add a few drops of mint-flavored chlorophyll. It is refreshing, hydrating, and oxygenating, and it helps with elimination.
- Check out *www.lborganic.com* regularly for updates and product recommendations.

I applaud your commitment to taking charge of your health by eating Super Enzyme Foods and choosing to Live Beyond Organic. Whether your concern is weight loss, detoxification, or dis-ease prevention, I know you will benefit from this lifestyle and achieve positive results.

With the information in these pages you can enjoy life-infusing meals that restore balance to your body and improve the quality of your life.

| **YOU** can do it! |

21-DAY
Beyond Organic
MENU PLAN

Day 1

BREAKFAST

1 cup fresh papaya with 1 teaspoon lemon juice
1 cup Papua New Guinea Coffee (*see recipe on page 180*),
   Thyme Tea Infusion (*see recipe on page 205*),
   or goat's milk
1 whole wheat English muffin, toasted
2 tablespoons soft goat's cheese
1 teaspoon raw honey

SNACK

12 whole Raw Soaked Almonds (*see recipe on page 186*)
1 small pear
¼ cup sunflower sprouts

LUNCH

Beyond Organic Sandwich (*see recipe on page 137*)
Sereni-Tea Blend or Thyme Tea Infusion

SNACK

2 organic whole wheat graham crackers
1 cup goat's milk

DINNER

6-8 ounce Salmon Ponzu (*see recipe on page 192*)
¾ cup Savory Brown Rice (*see recipe on page 194*)
2 cups Baby Spinach Salad with Creamy Lemon Dressing
   (*see recipes on pages 132 and 156*)
1 serving Berry Medley Sorbet (*see recipe on page 134*)

Day 2

BREAKFAST

8-ounce Tropical Smoothie (*see recipe on page 207*)
Scrumptious Hash Browns (*see recipe on page 195*)
1 cup Papua New Guinea Coffee (*see recipe on page 180*)
   or Thyme Tea Infusion (*see recipe on page 205*)

SNACK

Almond Butter & Honey (AB&H) Sandwich
   (the antidote to peanut butter and jelly)
   (*see recipe on page 124*)
8 ounce goat's milk or Thyme Tea Infusion

LUNCH

2 cups California Salad (*see recipe on page 153*)
¼ cup Simple Dressing (*see recipe on page 196*)
2 whole grain crackers (optional)

SNACK

1 Stuffed Roma or Heirloom Tomato
   (*see recipe on page 202*)
¼ cup alfalfa sprouts

DINNER

1 cup Bison Pennagna (*see recipe on page 144*)
1 cup steamed broccoli with lemon zest
1 slice Toasted Elephant Bread (*see recipe on page 206*)
¾ cup coconut, rice, or soy milk ice cream
Organic chocolate syrup

Day 3

BREAKFAST

1 cup fresh raspberries, blackberries, or strawberries
½ cup Brown Rice Farina with Dates and Cream
   (*see recipe on page 151*)
1 cup Papua New Guinea Coffee (*see recipe on page 180*)
   or Thyme Tea Infusion (*see recipe on page 205*)

SNACK

½ cup Berry Trail Mix (*see recipe on page 137*)
1 cup goat's yogurt (optional)

LUNCH

4 Egg Salad Triangles (*see recipe on page 158*)
¼ cup broccoli sprouts
1 kiwi

SNACK

1 cup broccoli or cauliflower florets
Herb Dip (*see recipe on page 172*)

DINNER

Gourmet Grilled Shrimp (*see recipe on page 169*)
2 cups Baby Spring Mix Salad (*see recipe on page 132*)
½ cup Balsamico Dressing (*see recipe on page 133*)
Tangerines with Honey Yogurt Sauce
   (*see recipe on page 205*)

Day 4

BREAKFAST

1 cup fresh pineapple
1 whole wheat English muffin, toasted
1 tablespoon goat's butter
1 teaspoon brown rice syrup
1 cup Papua New Guinea Coffee (*see recipe on page 180*)
Organic heavy cream and Sucanat (optional)

SNACK

1 cup goat's milk or Sereni-tea
2 Mocha Cookies (*see recipe on page 176*)

LUNCH

Salmon Salad Sandwich (Super Alternative to tuna)
    (*see recipe on page 193*)
Spicy Lemonade (*see recipe on page 198*)

SNACK

Belgian endive with goat's cheese Herb Dip
    (*see recipe on page 172*)

DINNER

Bison Tacarito (*see recipe on page 146*)
Red clover sprouts
Spicy Mango Salsa and Guacamole Fantastico!
    (*see recipes on pages 199 and 171*)
Organic corn chips
Cinnamon Krispies (*see recipe on page 156*)

Day 5

BREAKFAST

½ ripe Hawaiian papaya

Sunshine in a Slice (*see recipe on page 202*)

1 cup Papua New Guinea Coffee (*see recipe on page 180*)
   or Te de Canella (cinnamon stick tea) with goat's milk
   and maple syrup (*see recipe on page 205*)

SNACK

½ cup raw cashews

¼ cup red raisins

LUNCH

1 Red Bean Burrito (*see recipe on page 186*)

¼ cup goat's Gouda cheese, grated

¼ cup red clover sprouts

1 cup dark grapes (red, blue, black)

SNACK

12 organic corn chips

½ cup Spicy Mango Salsa (*see recipe on page 199*)

DINNER

Trout with Herbed Butter (*see recipe on page 208*)

1 cup Green Beans Almandine (*see recipe on page 170*)

1 cup Cucumber, Avocado, and Beet Salad
   (*see recipe on page 157*)

1 slice EZ Yam Custard Pie (*see recipe on page 163*)

1 dollop fresh whipped cream (optional)

Day 6

BREAKFAST

1 cup honeydew melon
1 slice sprouted barley bread, toasted
1 tablespoon Fruity Cheese Spread
   (*see recipe on page 166*)
1 cup Papua New Guinea Coffee
   (*see recipe on page 180*)

SNACK

1 cup cantaloupe sprinkled with RealSalt

LUNCH

1 Basic Bison Burger (*see recipe on page 133*)
Pineapple Soda (*see recipe on page 181*)

SNACK

1 pear, quartered
2 slices Manchego cheese
¼ cup sunflower sprouts

DINNER

Udon Tossed with Asparagus and Elephant Garlic Butter
   (*see recipe on page 210*)
Spinach Salad with Crimini Mushrooms
   (*see recipe on page 200*)
   and Honey Mustard Dressing (*see recipe on page 174*)
1 piece Pineapple Upside-Down Cake
   (*see recipe on page 181*)

Day 7

BREAKFAST

½ ripe Hawaiian papaya
Ara's Ducks and Dates (*see recipe on page 128*)
2 4-inch whole wheat lavash squares (flatbread)
1 cup Papua New Guinea Coffee (*see recipe on page 180*)
   or 1 cup goat's milk

SNACK

Red Potato Flower Salad (*see recipe on page 189*)

LUNCH

Grilled Gouda Sandwich (*see recipe on page 170*)

SNACK

Crudités with Herb Dip (*see recipe on page 157*)

DINNER

1-2 cups Osekihan (brown rice with red kidney beans)
   (*see recipe on page 177*)
Mandarin Salad (*see recipe on page 175*)
1 cup Fruit Crisp (*see recipe on page 165*)

Day 8

BREAKFAST

6-ounce Berry Smoothie (*see recipe on page 136*)
1 cup organic shredded wheat cereal
1 cup goat's milk
1 cup Sereni-tea or Chamomile/Peppermint Tea Infusion
   (*see recipe on page 155*)

SNACK

Yam Chips (*see recipe on page 213*)
Goat's milk

LUNCH

Avocado, Arugula, and Sprout Roll-Up
   (*see recipe on page 130*)

SNACK

1-3 organic whole wheat graham crackers
1 8-ounce glass goat's milk

DINNER

2-4 Bison Lettuce Wraps with spicy dipping sauce
   (*see recipe on page 142*)
Berry Parfait (*see recipe on page 136*)

Day 9

BREAKFAST

1 cup fresh raspberries
1 half sprouted wheat bagel, lightly toasted
2 tablespoons Fruity Cheese Spread
    (*see recipe on page 166*)
1 cup Papua New Guinea Coffee (*see recipe on page 180*)
Organic heavy cream and Sucanat (optional)

SNACK

1 cup Vanilla Yogurt (*see recipe on page 211*)

LUNCH

1 English Muffin Pizza (*see recipe on page 160*)
Raw broccoli florets with ¼ cup Guacamole Fantastico!
    (*see recipe on page 171*)

SNACK

Fresh Pineapple Triangles (*see recipe on page 164*)
Wheat berry sprouts with RealSalt

DINNER

6-8 ounces Omani orange roughy
1-2 cups brown rice
Herb salad with jicama
1 slice Pink Pear Pie (*see recipe on page 182*)

Day 10

BREAKFAST

Papaya Smoothie (*see recipe on page 178*)
Papua New Guinea Coffee (*see recipe on page 180*)
1 cup Pommes a la Christara (Lavender Potatoes)
    (*see recipe on page 184*)

SNACK

1 Fruity Banana Split (*see recipe on page 166*)

LUNCH

Wild Lox and Bagel (*see recipe on page 212*)
1 cup cantaloupe pieces sprinkled with RealSalt

SNACK

Raw green beans sprinkled with RealSalt

DINNER

1 slice The Ultimate Quiche (*see recipe on page 210*)
1-2 cups California Salad (*see recipe on page 153*)
2 bite-size dark chocolate pieces with fresh mint leaves
1 6-ounce glass goat's milk

Day 11

BREAKFAST

2 Super Pancakes (*see recipe on page 203*)
1 cup fresh berries
2 tablespoons Grade B maple syrup
1 cup Papua New Guinea Coffee (*see recipe on page 180*)
    or goat's milk

SNACK

½ avocado with
2 tablespoons first cold-pressed (FCP) extra virgin olive oil,
    Balsamic vinegar, a dash of RealSalt and cayenne

LUNCH

1-2 cups Red Potato Leek Soup (*see recipe on page 189*)

SNACK

7 raw asparagus stalks with dash of RealSalt
1-2 cups Thyme Tea Infusion (*see recipe on page 205*)

DINNER

2 pieces Bison Cutlets (*see recipe on page 141*)
1 cup Baby Lima Bean Rice (*see recipe on page 131*)
1 cup goat's yogurt with crookneck squash
4 cucumber spears with lemon juice and RealSalt
1 glass Chocolage (*see recipe on page 155*)

Day 12

BREAKFAST

½ fresh Hawaiian papaya
1 teaspoon lemon juice
1 organic whole grain waffle
2 teaspoons Grade B maple syrup
6 ounces goat's milk or Thyme Tea Infusion
  (*see recipe on page 205*)

SNACK

1 Brown Rice Cake
  (*available at health food and vitamin stores*)
1 tablespoon raw Almond Butter (*see recipe on page 124*)
1 teaspoon raw wild honey and cinnamon

LUNCH

1 Bison Cutlet Sandwich (*see recipe on page 140*)
  with sprouts
2 glasses Spicy Lemonade (*see recipe on page 198*)

SNACK

1 cup jicama sticks
¼ cup Herb Dip (*see recipe on page 172*)

DINNER

2 cups Eggplant Spaghetti (*see recipe on page 159*)
Caprese Salad (*see recipe on page 153*)
2 pieces Toasted Elephant Bread (*see recipe on page 206*)
1 cup Black Cherry Blender Ice Cream
  (*see recipe on page 147*)

Day 13

BREAKFAST

1 cup goat's milk
Blackberry Breakfast Krisp (*see recipe on page 148*)
Papua New Guinea Coffee (*see recipe on page 180*)

SNACK

Fresh mango slices sprinkled with RealSalt
　　and cayenne pepper

LUNCH

Enzymatic tabouli
1 whole wheat pita or lavash, toasted

SNACK

1 cup raw beet sticks
¼ cup Herb Dip (*see recipe on page 172*)

DINNER

Bison Loaf (*see recipe on page 143*)
2 cups Arugula, Pear, and Manchego Salad
　　(*see recipe on page 130*)
½ cup Simple Dressing (*see recipe on page 196*)
1 glass Chocolate Milk (*see recipe on page 155*)

Day 14

BREAKFAST

½ Hawaiian papaya
1 cup Tortilla Egg Scramble (*see recipe on page 206*)
Fresh salsa or cayenne pepper
Te de Canela (Cinnamon Stick Tea)
   (*see recipe on page 205*)

SNACK

1 cup organic crispy brown rice cereal with ½ cup goat's
   milk and a dash of cinnamon

LUNCH

Gouda Cheese Quesadilla (*see recipe on page 168*)
   with fresh guacamole

SNACK

2 slices whole wheat baguette
2 tablespoons Black Olive Tapenade
   (*see recipe on page 148*)

DINNER

½-1 cup Bison Chili (*see recipe on page 138*)
1-2 cups Quick Fries (*see recipe on page 185*)
1 cup Enzymatic Shirazi Salad (*see recipe on page 161*)
Lemon dressing
Chamomile/Peppermint Tea Infusion
   (*see recipe on page 155*) and dates

Day 15

BREAKFAST

1 banana, sliced
1 cup Organic Corn Flakes with 1 cup goat's milk
Papua New Guinea Coffee or Thyme Tea Infusion
    with raw honey (*see recipes on pages 180 and 205*)

SNACK

8 cucumber spears with lemon juice and RealSalt
2-4 organic whole-grain crackers

LUNCH

1 cup Bison Chili and Lace (*see recipe on page 139*),
    garnished with
½ cup fresh Roma tomatoes
½ avocado
1 tablespoon fresh basil leaves, chopped

SNACK

½ whole-wheat pita
1 ounce French feta cheese
½ cup broccoli spouts drizzled with
1 tablespoon FCP olive oil and
Dash RealSalt and cayenne pepper

DINNER

2 cups Seven Veggie Soba (*see recipe on page 196*)
Almond Cookies (*see recipe on page 125*)

Day 16

BREAKFAST

1 cup fresh pineapple
1 hard-boiled duck egg mashed with 1 teaspoon goat's butter
RealSalt and cayenne pepper to taste served on
½ whole-wheat English muffin, toasted
1 cup Papua New Guinea Coffee (*see recipe on page 180*)
   with cream and Sucanat to taste

SNACK

½ avocado with 2 tablespoons FCP extra virgin olive oil with
1 teaspoon fresh lemon juice RealSalt and cayenne pepper
   to taste
2 whole grain crackers

LUNCH

Baby Spinach Salad (*see recipe on page 132*)
   with Honey Mustard Dressing (*see recipe on page 174*)

SNACK

12 ounce Black Cherry Smoothie
   (*see recipe on page 147*)

DINNER

6-8 ounce Iron-Roasted Salmon (*see recipe on page 174*)
1-2 cups Savory Brown Rice (*see recipe on page 194*)
Raw organic broccoli
1 slice Chacocoban Cake (*see recipe on page 154*)

Day 17

BREAKFAST

6-ounce Tropical Smoothie (*see recipe on page 207*)
Scrumptious French Toast (*see recipe on page 195*)
Papua New Guinea Coffee (*see recipe on page 180*)
    or goat's milk

SNACK

½ Stuffed Avocado (*see recipe on page 201*)
1 tablespoon crumbled feta cheese
1 small Roma tomato, chopped
2 tablespoon FCP extra virgin olive oil

LUNCH

1 cup Broccoli Fennel Soup (*see recipe on page 150*)
2 whole-grain crackers

SNACK

1 slice day-old Chacocoban Cake (*see recipe on page 154*)
1 cup goat's milk

DINNER

Bison Teriyaki (*see recipe on page 146*)
Savory Brown Rice (*see recipe on page 194*)
    tossed with raw kale and fennel bulb
Pears with Chocolate Sauce (*see recipe on page 180*)

Day 18

BREAKFAST

1 cup papaya
1 Almond Spice Muffin (*see recipe on page 126*)
Thyme Tea Infusion (*see recipe on page 205*)
    or goat's milk

SNACK

1 cup raw beets
¼ cup Herb Dip (*see recipe on page 172*)

LUNCH

1 Salad-Stuffed Whole-Wheat Pita and Creamy Lemon
    Dressing (*see recipes on pages 191 and 156*)

SNACK

½ cup fresh/frozen organic black cherries

DINNER

1 Red Enchilada (*see recipe on page 187*)
½ cup Spanish rice (optional)
2 cups Baby Spring Mix Salad (*see recipe on page 132*)
Avocado Dressing (*see recipe on page 131*)
Frozen Mango Delight (*see recipe on page 165*)

Day 19

BREAKFAST

1 Simple Scramble (*see recipe on page 197*)
1 slice sprouted barley toast, buttered
1 cup Papua New Guinea Coffee (*see recipe on page 180*)
Cream and Sucanat to taste

SNACK

1 cup Yam Chips (*see recipe on page 213*)
¼ cup Herb Dip (*see recipe on page 172*)

LUNCH

1 cup Amazing Three-Layer Dip (*see recipe on page 127*)
1 cup Sprouted Corn Chips (*see recipe on page 200*)

SNACK

1 cup fresh pineapple

DINNER

1-2 cups Red Rice with Bison (*see recipe on page 190*)
Cucumber spears with lemon juice and RealSalt
1 cup yogurt and cucumber
Hibiscus tea and dried figs

Day 20

BREAKFAST

½ toasted whole wheat English muffin
½ avocado and crumbled feta cheese; 2 tablespoons
  FCP extra virgin olive oil; RealSalt and cayenne pepper
  to taste
1 cup Thyme Tea Infusion (*see recipe on page 205*)
  with raw honey to taste

SNACK

1 cup fresh strawberries, raspberries, or blackberries

LUNCH

1 bowl Red Lentil Soup (*see recipe on page 188*)
½ pita, toasted

SNACK

1 small pear

DINNER

Udon n'Cheese (*see recipe on page 208*)
  tossed with Fresh Broccoli
Arugula, Avocado, and Fennel Salad
  (*see recipe on page 129*)
2 Mocha Cookies (*see recipe on page 176*)

Day 21

BREAKFAST

½ Hawaiian papaya

Hot brown rice cereal with milled flax seed
   (*see recipe on page 151*)

Papua New Guinea Coffee (*see recipe on page 180*)
   with organic heavy cream and Sucanat

SNACK

2 cups Good Old-Fashioned Popcorn
   (*see recipe on page 168*)

LUNCH

2 cups Wild Arugula Salad (*see recipe on page 211*)

½ cup Simple Dressing (*see recipe on page 196*)

4 Tamari brown rice crackers

SNACK

1 cup honeydew melon

DINNER

Pan-Broiled Wasabi Salmon (*see recipe on page 178*)

1 cup brown rice with Udon*

Mandarin Salad (*see recipe on page 175*)

3 rings dried pineapple

Chamomile Tea Infusion (*see recipe on page 154*)

ReCipes

Life events focus on our food,
so our food must enhance our life.

*Living Beyond Organic Herb Blends that
I use in my recipes are available at
www.LBOrganic.com.*

ALMOND BUTTER

1 pound raw almonds
½ teaspoon cinnamon
½ teaspoon cardamom
½ teaspoon fennel powder
½ teaspoon FCP extra virgin olive oil (if needed)
Dash of RealSalt

Pour almonds into food processor, grind to a meal consistency then add cinnamon, cardamom, and fennel. Continue grinding until mixture turns to a creamy consistency. This sometimes requires adding olive oil. Once you are satisfied with the consistency, store almond butter in a glass container with a tight-fitting lid. Must be refrigerated, and will stay fresh for 1 week. Excellent to have on hand for a quick snack or school lunch. I like to use it in my bison chili. Enjoy!

ALMOND BUTTER & HONEY (AB&H) SANDWICH

2 slices sprouted barley bread
¼ cup almond butter
1 tablespoon raw honey
¼ teaspoon cinnamon
½ cup fresh raspberries, blackberries, or strawberries

Mix almond butter and honey with cinnamon; spread mixture on bread and cover with other slice. Cut into quarters on diagonal, and enjoy each tasty piece. Serve berries on the side.

ALMOND BUTTER & HONEY SNACK

1 slice barley bread, toasted
¼ cup almond butter
¼ teaspoon cinnamon
½ cup fresh raspberries or blackberries
1 tablespoon raw honey

Lightly toast bread, spread with almond butter, and sprinkle with cinnamon. Garnish with fresh berries and drizzle with raw honey.

ALMOND COOKIES

2 cups whole-wheat pastry flour
1 teaspoon baking powder (alum free)
⅔ cup organic unsalted butter
1 medium duck egg white (reserve yolk)
1½ cups Sucanat
2 teaspoons organic almond extract
1 medium duck egg yolk (beaten)
24 whole raw almonds (reserve for garnish)
¼ teaspoon RealSalt
Dash cardamom

In a medium mixing bowl, combine butter and Sucanat with a pastry cutter until blended; whisk in egg, almond extract, cardamom, and salt. Combine flour and baking powder; add to butter mixture. Mix well with a pastry cutter. Form cookie dough rolls; place on unbleached waxed paper; roll up and place in plastic wrap; chill until ready to use. Preheat oven to 375 degrees. Cut chilled dough into 1-inch-thick slices; place on baking stone or stainless-steel cookie sheet. Whisk egg, cardamom, and salt together. Garnish with an almond and brush with egg yolk. Bake at 375 for 15 minutes or until golden brown.

ALMOND SPICE MUFFINS

1 cup whole-wheat pastry flour
½ cup barley flour
1 duck egg
1 cup Sucanat
1 cup raw almond milk or goat's milk
1 teaspoon baking powder
1 cup almond pulp or ground almonds
1 teaspoon cinnamon, ground
¼ teaspoon nutmeg (optional)
1 tablespoon safflower oil

Preheat oven to 375 degrees. Combine egg, almond milk or goat's milk, pulp or ground almonds, Sucanat, and spices; mix well. Mix flour and dry ingredients. Add flour mixture to milk mixture, and mix until blended. If batter is too thick, add milk; if too liquid, add flour. Grease baking pans with safflower oil and pour in batter. Bake for approximately 30 minutes or until done (test center with wooden toothpick). Quick shortcut for this recipe: place soaked almonds in the blender with goat's milk and puree to a smooth consistency. Follow recipe as directed.

AMAZING THREE-LAYER DIP

1 can organic red kidney beans
1 ounce organic heavy cream
1 tablespoon safflower oil
1 teaspoon RealSalt
1 teaspoon dried oregano
1 teaspoon lecithin powder (non-GMO)
1 large avocado
1 lime, cut in half
1 tablespoon elephant garlic, grated
2 Roma tomatoes
1 slice red onion, chopped
¼ cup fresh cilantro, chopped
½ cup FCP extra virgin olive oil
Cayenne pepper to taste
½ cup Daisy sour cream

Rinse beans with fresh water; drain. Heat oil in a heavy skillet and add beans, cream, oregano, and salt. Mash to consistency desired. For smoother texture, add lecithin powder. Spread beans in a glass serving dish. Combine avocado, half the garlic, half the lime juice, half the olive oil, and a dash of salt with a fork. Spread over the beans. Then combine tomatoes and cilantro with remaining lime juice, olive oil, and salt. Add cayenne pepper to taste. Stir and pour over avocado. Garnish with dollops of sour cream.

ANTIOXIDANT SANDWICH SPREAD

½ cup Daisy sour cream or crème fraîche
1 tablespoon raw beet, grated
1 tablespoon horseradish, finely grated
2 tablespoons FCP extra virgin olive oil
¼ teaspoon RealSalt

In a small mixing bowl combine ingredients and stir well; use in place of mayo for a new taste experience to your sandwiches. An excellent way to incorporate raw beets and horseradish into your diet. Can be prepared in advance and refrigerated. Best used within 72 hours to receive maximum enzymatic properties.

ARA'S DUCKS AND DATES

2 medium duck eggs
4 pitted Medjool dates, halved
2 tablespoons organic unsalted butter
½ teaspoon RealSalt
Dash cayenne pepper

Cut dates in half, remove the pits, and set aside. In a heavy skillet, melt butter over a medium flame; add dates and lightly brown on one side. Use long tongs to turn over the dates, and arrange them in a circular pattern on the outer edges of the skillet. Dates cook very quickly and can burn; if necessary, remove the dates from the skillet and set aside. If needed, add more butter. Crack eggs one at a time into a glass measuring cup, then pour into the center of the pan. Cover and cook about 1 minute or until eggs are done sunny side up. (If your egg yolks break or you prefer scrambled, use a spatula to simply fold the eggs and dates together until eggs are cooked.) Place eggs and dates in a piece of whole-wheat lavash or whole-wheat pita bread. Fold in half and get ready for a new taste experience.

This dish is best served immediately eaten one bite at a time. Take a small piece of bread and arrange a bite-size portion of egg and date on top.

ARUGULA, AVOCADO, AND FENNEL SALAD

    4 cups arugula
    2 avocados, peeled and sliced
    1 fennel bulb, thinly sliced
    ¼ teaspoon RealSalt
    ¼ cup pine nuts (optional)

Rinse arugula in water with 1 drop food-grade hydrogen peroxide. Place in salad spinner to extract excess water. Place in
a mixing bowl and refrigerate to keep crisp.

In a separate bowl, combine avocado and fennel slices;
sprinkle with RealSalt and 1 teaspoon lemon juice. Combine
mixture with arugula; toss well with dressing, and garnish
with pine nuts. Serve immediately.

Dressing

    ¼ cup FCP extra virgin olive oil
    2 tablespoons fresh squeezed lemon juice
    ¼ teaspoon thyme
    ¼ teaspoon marjoram
    ½ teaspoon elephant garlic, grated
    ¼ teaspoon lecithin powder (non-GMO)
    ¼ teaspoon RealSalt
    Dash cayenne pepper

Combine all ingredients in blender or food processor until
smooth. This can be prepared in advance and refrigerated.
Use within 24 hours.

This dressing is also delicious as a sauce over chilled
salmon, garnished with avocado slices.

ARUGULA, PEAR, AND MANCHEGO SALAD

2 cups organic arugula
2 tablespoons raw almonds, sliced
12 slices Manchego cheese
1 medium pear, thinly sliced
¼ cup FCP extra virgin olive oil
1 medium lemon, juiced
2 thin slices elephant garlic
1 teaspoon almonds, ground
½ teaspoon lecithin powder
½ teaspoon Kal Nutritional Yeast
½ teaspoon RealSalt
Dash cayenne pepper

Rinse arugula, using a salad spinner or patting dry on paper towels. In a large salad bowl combine arugula, pear, cheese, and almonds (reserve 1 teaspoon). In a food processor combine olive oil, lemon juice, reserved almonds, garlic, nutritional yeast, and salt; blend until smooth. Drizzle over salad, toss well, and serve.

AVOCADO, ARUGULA, AND SPROUT ROLL-UP

1 Ezekiel sprouted grain tortilla
½ avocado, ripe
1 cup wild arugula
½ cup alfalfa sprouts
2 tablespoons FCP extra virgin olive oil
RealSalt and cayenne pepper to taste

In a medium stainless-steel skillet warm tortilla on each side and place on a cutting board. Layer slices of avocado onto tortilla; add arugula and your favorite sprouts. Drizzle with olive oil; salt and pepper to taste. Roll up, cut in half, and serve with your favorite fruit. Enjoy!

AVOCADO DRESSING

1 whole avocado
½ cup FCP extra virgin olive oil
2 tablespoons fresh lemon juice
1 teaspoon All Purpose Herb Blend
1 teaspoon elephant garlic freshly grated
  or ½ teaspoon Garlic Blend
½ teaspoon RealSalt
Dash cayenne pepper

Cut avocado in half lengthwise; remove pit and discard. Gently scoop out avocado and place in blender or food processor; add remaining ingredients and blend for 30 seconds until smooth. Refrigerate until ready to use. This is a great way to get your daily serving of avocado. Less filling too!

BABY LIMA BEAN RICE

4 cups brown basmati rice, cooked
2 cups baby lima beans, frozen
1 cup fresh dill, chopped
3 tablespoons dried dill
3 tablespoons organic unsalted butter bits
1 teaspoon RealSalt
2 medium sliced red potatoes or whole-wheat lavash
¼ cup safflower oil
3 sprigs fresh dill (optional)
2 tablespoons grape seed oil (optional)
3 sprigs fresh dill (reserve for garnish)

In large mixing bowl combine rice, lima beans, dill, and salt; toss well. Coat the bottom of a large pot with oil; heat over medium flame, and line bottom of pot with potato slices or lavash. Pour rice mixture into the pot and top with butter bits. Cover and simmer for 25 minutes. When done, rice is hot and steamy, lima beans are tender, and the potatoes are nicely browned.

This dish is an excellent vegetarian entrée and also is a delicious accompaniment to your favorite fish and bison dishes.

BABY SPINACH SALAD

6 ounce bag baby spinach
1 beet, shredded
¼ small red onion, finely sliced
1 large avocado, cubed
1 medium Heirloom or 2 Roma tomatoes, chopped
1 medium Persian cucumber, peeled and sliced

Rinse spinach leaves well with 1 drop food-grade hydrogen peroxide. Place in salad spinner to remove excess moisture. Place in chilled salad bowl; add tomato, cucumber, beet, and avocado. Toss well with Balsamico Dressing (*see page 133*). Keep chilled until ready to serve.

BABY SPRING MIX SALAD

6 ounces Spring Mix
2 Roma tomatoes, chopped
2 cucumbers, chopped
1 small beet, shredded
¼ small red onion, thinly sliced

Rinse salad leaves well with 1 drop food-grade hydrogen peroxide. Place in salad spinner to remove excess moisture. Place in chilled salad bowl; add tomato, cucumber, beet, and red onion. Toss well with Balsamico Dressing (*see page 133*). Chill until ready to serve.

living beyond organic

BALSAMICO DRESSING

½ cup FCP extra virgin olive oil
¼ cup balsamic vinegar
1 teaspoon organic mustard
1 teaspoon elephant garlic, pressed
1 teaspoon Kal Nutritional Yeast Flakes
Dash RealSalt and cayenne pepper

Place all ingredients in a mixing bowl and whisk briskly. Place in a glass bottle or jar with tight-fitting lid. Refrigerate until ready to use.

BASIC BISON BURGER

1 pound ground bison
1 Roma tomato
¼ cup organic tamari
1 tablespoon All Purpose Herb Blend
1 teaspoon Garlic Blend
1 teaspoon paprika

- or -

¼ cup fresh basil leaves (optional) or 1 teaspoon dried basil
½ teaspoon dried thyme
½ teaspoon fennel, ground
1 tablespoon elephant garlic, pressed
1 tablespoon organic safflower or sunflower oil
Dash cayenne pepper

Place bison in a glass or stainless-steel mixing bowl and set aside. Combine tomato, garlic, tamari, herbs and spices in a blender or food processor. Add puréed mixture to bison and mix well. Shape into patties. Preheat a cast iron or stainless-steel skillet over medium flame; season with safflower oil. Cook 5 minutes per side for medium or until desired doneness is achieved. Makes four burger patties.

Patties can be frozen when raw. To freeze wrap them individually in unbleached parchment and place in heavy-duty plastic freezer bags. Use within 3 weeks if stored in a frostless freezer, up to 6 months in a deep freeze.

BASIC PIECRUST

1¼ cups whole-wheat pastry flour
3 tablespoons organic unsalted butter
2-3 tablespoons safflower oil
2-3 tablespoons iced natural spring water

In a stainless-steel or glass bowl cut butter into flour with a pastry cutter. Gradually add oil while you continue mixing to crumbly consistency. Gradually add ice water, while mixing until you reach a dough consistency. Make a ball and place on floured unbleached parchment paper. Flatten dough with your hand and sprinkle with flour. Place another sheet of unbleached wax paper over the dough and roll out to form a circle approximately 12-inches in diameter. Remove top layer of paper. Place buttered 9-inch pie plate over dough and turn plate, dough, and remaining piece of wax paper. Line pie plate with dough; flute edges or simply cut away excess dough with a knife. This pie crust is ready to be filled and baked or can be frozen for later use. To freeze, protect pie crust with a sheet of unbleached parchment paper and place in a large airtight freezer bag.

BERRY MEDLEY SORBET

2 cups organic frozen berries
1 cup goat's milk or almond milk
1 tablespoon Grade B maple syrup (optional)
¼ cup organic heavy cream (optional)
1 teaspoon lecithin powder (non-GMO)

Place half of the almond milk in a blender. Slowly add frozen berries until you reach desired consistency. For a thicker consistency add more frozen berries; for a liquid consistency add more almond milk. To sweeten, add maple syrup; for a creamy texture, add cream. Serve immediately.

You can use your favorite frozen fruit with this recipe. My favorite is organic black cherry.

Note: If using fresh fruit, add ice cubes to thicken the consistency.

| A REFRESHING ANTI-OXIDANT |

BERRY PARFAIT

12 ounces mixed blackberries, raspberries, and strawberries

1 tablespoon Absolut vodka (optional)

1 cup Fresh Whipped Cream (*see recipe on page 164*)

2 tablespoons fructose

¼ cup organic chocolate chips
   or ½ cup organic chocolate syrup

Thoroughly rinse and pat dry berries. Refrigerate until ready to use. If desired, toss with vodka and 1 teaspoon fructose, and chill. To whip cream by hand, combine ½ cup heavy cream with 1 tablespoon fructose and whisk briskly for about 3 minutes or until cream peaks.

In a chilled parfait glass, layer a dollop of whipped cream followed by berries, alternating until the glass is filled. Garnish with chocolate chips or syrup. Serve immediately.

BERRY SMOOTHIE

1 pound blackberries, frozen

1 cup goat's milk

½ cup goat's yogurt

2 tablespoons Grade B maple syrup

1 tablespoon lecithin powder

Place milk and yogurt in blender. Add half the blackberries and blend on high. Next add maple syrup and lecithin powder. Add more berries if a thicker consistency is desired.

BERRY TRAIL MIX

    12 ounces raw almonds

    12 ounces raw cashews

    8 ounces organic dried cherries, cranberries, or mulberries
    (found in Middle Eastern markets)

    8 ounces organic dark chocolate chips (optional)

Combine all ingredients in a large bowl and mix well. Cover with tight-fitting lid. Keep refrigerated. I like to have this recipe ready for school snacks, long car trips, and hiking. This snack helps maintain your energy level and prevents you from overeating later.

BEYOND ORGANIC SANDWICH

    2 slices sprouted barley bread

    ½ avocado, thinly sliced

    1 Heirloom tomato, thinly sliced

    1 tablespoon fresh watercress

    1 tablespoon Beyond Organic Sandwich Spread
    (*see recipe below*)

Spread dressing on each slice of bread; layer with avocado, tomato, and watercress. Cover with bread slice and cut in half diagonally. Enjoy!

Note: Can be served open face (less filling). Also try it with alfalfa or broccoli sprouts!

BEYOND ORGANIC SANDWICH SPREAD

    ½ cup Daisy sour cream
    or crème fraîche

    1 teaspoon horseradish, freshly grated

    2 teaspoons beet, freshly grated

    Dash RealSalt and cayenne

Combine dressing ingredients and stir well. Use on sandwiches. Great as a sauce for chilled salmon and for dipping veggies!

BISON CHILI

1 pound fresh or frozen bison, ground

2 medium red onions, chopped

¾ cup safflower oil

1 32-ounce can organic Roma tomatoes

1 clove elephant garlic, pressed
   or 1 tablespoon Elephant Garlic Blend

1 cup dark red kidney beans, cooked (see below)
   or 1 can organic red kidney beans

3 tablespoons almonds, ground

1 tablespoon RealSalt

1 tablespoon organic chili powder
   or 1 teaspoon paprika and turmeric

1 teaspoon cumin, ground

1 teaspoon dried oregano

1 teaspoon dried thyme

1 teaspoon organic cacao powder

½ teaspoon cinnamon

1 teaspoon cayenne pepper (mild)
   or 1 tablespoon cayenne pepper (spicy)
   and 1 roasted Anaheim chili pepper, chopped

In a blender or food processor, blend tomatoes for 10 seconds and set aside. Mash beans and set aside. Combine all dried herbs and spices in a small bowl. Grate garlic and set aside. Heat ½ cup oil in large skillet; add onions and brown over a low flame until caramelized. This takes about 30 minutes, stirring and turning every 5 minutes, to prevent burning the onions. Remove from heat and set aside. In a large stainless-steel pot, heat remaining oil. Add ground bison in small chunks to cover bottom of pot, then add the herb and spice blend. With the edge of a spatula, chop meat and mix in grated garlic, herbs, and spices for 5 minutes or until cooked and evenly minced. Add tomatoes with liquid and mashed beans to thicken; add salt and stir over low flame for 5 minutes.

Optional: Roast Anaheim pepper on a grill or in a cast iron skillet, remove seeds, and chop into small pieces; combine with meat mixture. This adds extra flavor and heat to the chili. Serve with Quick Fries (*see recipe on page 185*).

BISON CHILI AND LACE

1 cup Bison Chili (*see recipe on page 138*)
1 medium red potato, grated
1 small garnet yam, grated
¼ cup safflower oil
½ teaspoon dried thyme
Dash cayenne pepper
¼ cup goat Gouda, grated (optional)
1 Roma tomato, chopped

Combine potato and yam in a mixing bowl; season with herbs and spices. Heat oil in a skillet over medium flame; layer potato/yam mixture in the skillet and cook until browned evenly on both sides. Lift the "lace" out with a stainless-steel spatula; drain on a paper towel and place on serving plate. Pour chili over lace; garnish with cheese and tomato. Serve with ½ avocado and 2 tablespoons FCP olive oil. This recipe is a tasty way to serve leftover chili; it's always better the next day!

BISON CUTLET SANDWICH

1 bison cutlet, cut lengthwise
1 Roma tomato, sliced
1 Persian cucumber, peeled and sliced
½ avocado, sliced
1 slice red onion (optional)
1 tablespoon FCP extra virgin olive oil
1 teaspoon lemon juice
RealSalt and cayenne pepper to taste
1 or 2 small square(s) wheat or barley lavash

Place bread on a plate. Arrange cutlet and veggies on the bread. Whisk oil in a small bowl with the juice; season with salt and pepper. Drizzle over sandwich ingredients, roll up, or fold bread over and enjoy.

This is the perfect meal to make with your leftover cutlets; it's like an entree and salad in one!

BISON CUTLETS

1 pound bison, ground
1 medium red onion, grated
2 small red potatoes, grated
1 clove elephant garlic, grated
1 cup cilantro, chopped
1 teaspoon turmeric
1 teaspoon dried thyme
1 teaspoon dried marjoram
1 teaspoon dried fennel, ground

Dredging

½ cup whole-wheat flour
3 cakes Weetabix, crumbled
1 teaspoon All Purpose Herb Blend
1 teaspoon RealSalt
Dash cayenne pepper
½ cup safflower oil

In a large mixing bowl, mix by hand the bison, onion, potato, garlic, turmeric, thyme, fennel, and marjoram. In a separate bowl combine flour, Weetabix, RealSalt, and cayenne pepper. Form the meat into oval patties about 3 inches long, and then dredge in flour mixture. Heat oil over medium flame in a large skillet; gently place patties into the skillet and cook until golden brown on each side. Do not overcook. With a spatula, remove cutlets from pan and place on a paper towel to absorb excess oil. Place cutlets in glass or ceramic bakeware and set aside. Bake uncovered in a preheated 375 degree oven for 20 minutes.

Cutlets can be served hot with brown basmati rice, yogurt, and cucumber spears with lemon juice and RealSalt or with Quick Fries (*see recipe on page 185*) and your favorite salad. Also great served cold, especially in sandwiches.

BISON LETTUCE WRAPS

1 pound ground bison
1 medium red onion, chopped
1 clove elephant garlic, grated
1 tablespoon fresh ginger root, grated
1 teaspoon dried thyme
$\frac{1}{4}$ cup safflower oil
$\frac{1}{4}$ cup tamari, reduced sodium
1 tablespoon Kal Nutritional Yeast Flakes
$\frac{1}{2}$ teaspoon cayenne pepper
$\frac{1}{4}$ teaspoon RealSalt
1 head butter lettuce, rinsed and chilled

Heat oil in a large skillet; add the onion and sauté until lightly browned. Add bison; mince meat with the onion, using the edge of a spatula. Continue cooking over medium flame while adding garlic, ginger, and dried thyme. Add tamari and cayenne pepper, and mix. During the last 5 minutes of cooking, add yeast flakes and salt to taste. Set aside until ready to serve.

Dipping Sauce

$\frac{1}{4}$ cup FCP extra virgin olive oil
$\frac{1}{4}$ cup raw wild honey
$\frac{1}{4}$ cup raw sliced almonds
1 teaspoon lecithin powder
1 tablespoon toasted elephant garlic
1 teaspoon cayenne pepper (you may wish to do this in
   $\frac{1}{2}$ teaspoon increments, tasting as you go)
$\frac{1}{4}$ teaspoon RealSalt

Combine all ingredients in a blender or food processor until smooth. Set aside in a gravy boat. After dipping sauce is prepared, arrange lettuce leaves on a platter and fill a large covered dish with meat mixture. Spoon the meat mixture onto leaves, drizzle with dipping sauce, and fold the leaf from the center upward to form a bottom and roll together from left to right. Arrange finished rolls on a platter and serve. I recommend having extra sauce ready at the table. For a small, casual gathering, it is fun to have everyone assemble their own. Enjoy!

BISON LOAF

2 pounds bison, ground
3 Italian eggplants, chopped
1 small red onion, chopped
1 cup leeks, thinly sliced
¼ cup Bragg Liquid Aminos or tamari
1 clove elephant garlic, grated
¼ cup safflower oil
1 duck egg, whisked
¼ cup organic heavy cream
¼ teaspoon RealSalt
1 cup organic whole-wheat breadcrumbs
  or 2 Weetabix biscuits, crumbled
2 cups fresh basil leaves

Preheat oven to 375 degrees. In a large stainless-steel skillet heat oil; add onion, eggplant, and leek; sauté until lightly browned. Reserve ¼ cup each of the onion and leek, and set aside for the topping sauce. Stir in grated garlic cover and set aside. Whisk egg and cream together in a small bowl. In a large glass or stainless mixing bowl, combine bison, liquid aminos, sautéed veggies and egg mixture; mix well. Add bread crumbs, milled flax, and RealSalt.

Place meat mixture on glass cutting board; press to spread meat onto board. Spread basil leaves onto meat. Roll meat into a loaf shape; invert baking dish over loaf and turn cutting board over to transfer loaf into baking dish. Re-shape loaf to an even 3-inch thickness so it will cook evenly. Place a sheet of unbleached parchment over loaf, cover baking dish with foil, and bake for 1 hour. While the loaf is baking start the topping sauce.

Bison-loaf Topping Sauce

3 Fresh Roma tomatoes, chopped
6 ounces sun-dried Roma tomatoes, hydrated and chopped
¾ cup boiled water
½ cup reserved onion/leek
¼ cup safflower oil

(*continued on page 144*)

BISON LOAF (continued)

¼ cup red wine (optional)

1 tablespoon Kal Nutritional Yeast Flakes (optional)

1 tablespoon Grade B maple syrup

1 tablespoon mustard, organic

1 teaspoon dried thyme

½ teaspoon cayenne pepper

In a small saucepan bring water to a boil. Add sun-dried Romas, cover the pan, and steep for 5 minutes. In a medium skillet, heat oil and sauté reserved onion and leek. Add chopped fresh and sun-dried tomatoes; cook approximately 5 minutes. Add mustard, maple syrup, dried thyme, cayenne pepper, and yeast flakes; stir over medium flame until blended. Pour evenly over loaf; top with a sheet of unbleached parchment, then tightly cover with foil and bake for the 20-30 minutes of cooking time remaining.

BISON PENNAGNA

1 pound ground bison

1 28-ounce can whole peeled Roma tomatoes

1 package sun-dried Roma tomatoes (hydrated)

¼ cup red wine (optional)

¼ cup safflower oil

1 teaspoon RealSalt

½ teaspoon cayenne pepper

½ cup Pecorino Romano cheese, grated (optional)

1 package (16 ounces) brown rice pasta

1 medium red onion, chopped

1 clove elephant garlic

1 teaspoon dried basil

1 teaspoon dried thyme

1 teaspoon fennel powder

1 teaspoon turmeric

¼ teaspoon cinnamon (optional)

2 Roma tomatoes, sliced

½ cup Pecorino Romano (sheep's cheese), grated

Meat Sauce

In large, heavy skillet heat oil over a medium flame, add onions, sauté until lightly browned. Add bison. Using the edge of a spatula, mince meat, and add in herbs and spices. Place sun-dried tomatoes in small saucepan, hydrate with a cup of boiled water, cover and steep for 15 minutes. Add canned Roma tomatoes; gently mash into meat mixture. In a blender combine sun-dried tomatoes and garlic for 30 seconds; add to meat mixture, stirring until well blended. Add red wine; simmer for 20 minutes. After cooking, add RealSalt and cayenne pepper.

Pasta

Fill a large pot with 7 cups of fresh water. Bring to a boil. Add pasta and cook approximately 10 minutes or until done. Take care not to overcook, especially when using brown rice pasta. Transfer cooked pasta into colander; drain excess water, pour pasta back into pot, and fold in meat sauce; combine well. Cover and set aside.

Cheese Filling

In a large mixing bowl whisk together

   8 ounces soft goat's cheese
   ½ cup organic heavy cream
   ½ cup Pecorino Romano, grated
   1 duck egg
   1 cup Gouda, grated
   1 cup fresh basil, chopped

Combine all ingredients in a mixing bowl and whisk until blended; fold in basil. Keep refrigerated until ready to use. Line the bottom of a large rectangular baking dish with a layer of pasta mixture, spread cheese mixture over the pasta, then add a second layer of pasta over the cheese. Top with 12 slices of Roma tomato and basil leaves and garnish with fresh grated Pecorino Romano. Cover dish with unbleached parchment paper, then with foil.

Preheat oven to 375 degrees. Bake at 375 degrees for 30 minutes. This dish can be prepared in advance and baked when needed.

BISON TACARITO

1 dozen organic whole-wheat-flour tortillas
2 cups Quick-Fried Beans (*see recipe on page 184*)
1 pound ground bison
½ cup safflower oil
1 red onion, chopped
1 tablespoon elephant garlic, grated
1 teaspoon cumin powder
1 teaspoon dried thyme
½ teaspoon turmeric
½ teaspoon cinnamon
½ teaspoon cayenne pepper
Dash of ground cloves (optional)
1 tablespoon Bragg Liquid Aminos or tamari, reduced sodium

In a large skillet, heat oil over medium flame. Add onion and cook until browned, stirring occasionally. This can take up to 30 minutes. Add ground bison, cumin, thyme, turmeric, cinnamon, and cayenne pepper. Using a spatula, mince the meat and mix the ingredients together; cook about 7 minutes. In the last minute of cooking, add grated garlic and Bragg Liquid Aminos. Remove from heat and set aside.

Prepare Quick-Fried Beans, Guacamole Fantasico!, Spicy Mango Salsa, and Sprouted Corn Chips (*see recipes on pages 184, 171, 199, 200*).

BISON TERIYAKI

1 pound bison tri-tip or sirloin thin strips
1 clove elephant garlic, grated
¼ cup fresh chives, chopped
1 tablespoon fresh ginger, grated
½ cup tamari, organic reduced sodium
¼ cup safflower oil
1 ounce Nigori Sake (optional)
¼ cup Grade B maple syrup
1 tablespoon organic cornstarch
1 tablespoon sesame seeds, roasted (for garnish)

¼ cup organic unsalted butter
¼ cup lemon juice
¼ cup fresh chives, chopped (for garnish)
Dash RealSalt and cayenne pepper

Pierce meat on all sides with a meat tenderizing tool, then cut into ¾-inch strips. Place strips in a bowl and toss with oil. Refrigerate until ready to cook. Preheat a large skillet and add sesame oil; stir-fry meat until done on all sides. Place cooked meat in serving dish and set aside. In the same skillet melt butter; add garlic, chives, ginger, tamari, maple syrup, lemon juice, and cayenne pepper. Thicken sauce with cornstarch. Continue stirring to desired thickness. Pour over bison strips, garnish with roasted sesame seeds and fresh chives. This recipe does not require prior marination.

BLACK CHERRY BLENDER ICE CREAM

1 16-ounce bag frozen organic black cherries
½ cup organic heavy cream
¼ cup Simple Syrup (*see recipe on page 197*)
   or Grade B maple syrup
1 teaspoon lecithin powder (non-GMO)
6 ice cubes

Place ingredients in blender; blend until smooth. Serve immediately.

BLACK CHERRY SMOOTHIE

1 cup organic black cherries, frozen
½ cup goat's or rice milk
1 tablespoon Grade B maple syrup
1 tablespoon goat's yogurt
1 teaspoon lecithin powder

Place all ingredients in blender; blend until smooth. To thicken mixture, add more frozen cherries or ice cubes. To liquefy the mixture, add more goat's milk. This recipe is so easy, satisfying, and good for you!

BLACK OLIVE TAPENADE

12 ounces black olives
1 tablespoon capers
1 tablespoon FCP extra virgin olive oil
1 teaspoon elephant garlic, pressed
1 teaspoon vodka (optional)
2 tablespoons organic heavy cream
1 teaspoon All Purpose Herb Blend
Dash RealSalt
Dash cayenne pepper

Combine all ingredients in a food processor until smooth. Pour into glass container with airtight lid and refrigerate until ready to use. Enjoy this recipe on lightly toasted baguette slices!

BLACKBERRY BREAKFAST KRISP

1 cup whole-wheat pastry flour
1 cup almonds, coarsely ground
1 cup New Morning graham crackers, crumbled
1 teaspoon cinnamon, ground
½ teaspoon cardamom, ground
¾ cup Sucanat
¼ pound organic unsalted butter, cut into bits
12 ounces blackberries, fresh or frozen
½ cup Grade B maple syrup
1 tablespoon organic cornstarch

Combine flour, almonds, graham crackers, cinnamon, cardamom, and Sucanat in a large mixing bowl, using your fingers. Then work in the butter until crumbly. Set aside. Combine berries, syrup, and cornstarch. Put ½ cup topping mixture into a glass mixing bowl and combine well with berries. Pour mixture into a round glass or porcelain baking dish. Top with remaining topping. Place on a stainless baking sheet on middle rack for 30 minutes at 375 degrees or until fruit is bubbling.

RICH IN VITAMIN E;
| PROTECTS HEALTHY CELLS |

BROCCOLI FENNEL SOUP

3 cups broccoli florets, finely chopped
1 small fennel bulb, chopped
1 small red onion, chopped
2 tablespoons safflower oil
½ teaspoon dried thyme
½ teaspoon turmeric
Dash cayenne pepper
1 tablespoon lecithin powder (non-GMO)
1 teaspoon RealSalt
½ cup almond milk or cream (optional)
4 cups natural spring water

In large pot heat oil over medium flame; add onion and fennel, and cook until lightly browned. Add herbs, spices, and water. Bring to a boil; reduce heat and simmer for 10 minutes. Remove from heat. With a slotted spoon, separate cooked solids into the blender. Add almond milk, lecithin powder, cayenne pepper, and salt; blend until smooth. Stir mixture into soup over low flame; for a creamy texture try adding shredded goat's Gouda cheese. Stir in finely chopped raw broccoli. Garnish with olive oil and a dash of cayenne pepper. Enjoy!

BROWN RICE FARINA WITH DATES AND CREAM

½ cup brown rice cereal

1½ cups natural spring water

¼ teaspoon organic vanilla extract, alcohol-free

¼ teaspoon cinnamon

Dash RealSalt to taste after cooking

1 tablespoon Sucanat or Grade B maple syrup

¼ cup organic heavy cream, goat's milk, or fresh almond milk

¼ cup dates, chopped or 1 tablespoon milled flax seed

In a saucepan bring water to a boil. Stir in cereal, vanilla, and cinnamon. Lower heat; cover and cook about 5 minutes, stirring occasionally. Add dash of RealSalt once the cereal is cooked. Serve with heavy cream, goat's milk, or almond milk. Try variations of this recipe with your favorite dried fruit.

BROWN RICE PUDDING

6 cups goat's milk

1 cup organic brown rice (short grain)

½ cup Sucanat

½ teaspoon cinnamon

1 tablespoon organic vanilla extract
  or ½ teaspoon vanilla bean

1 teaspoon lecithin powder

In a medium saucepan add milk and rice. Bring to a boil; reduce heat and simmer for 45 minutes or until rice is cooked. Next add Sucanat, cinnamon, vanilla, and lecithin powder, stirring continuously until thickened. Pour into glass dish and refrigerate 3 hours. Spoon mixture into parfait glasses, and garnish with dried fruit and cinnamon. For variety try this recipe with dried currants, red raisins, chopped apricots or dates, and, of course, Fresh Whipped Cream (*see recipe on page 164*).

BROWNIES BY TIARA

1 box Natures Path Organic Double Fudge Brownie Mix
5 dates, chopped
4 tablespoons safflower oil or organic unsalted butter
½ cup natural spring water or goat's milk
1 tablespoon milled flaxseed
1 teaspoon organic vanilla extract
Dash of cinnamon

Preheat oven to 350. Mix all ingredients in a glass or stainless-steel mixing bowl. Pour into lightly oiled pan (safflower oil); bake for 40 minutes and you have yummy brownies.

I like to make brownie parfaits. It's easy! Just layer crumbled brownies with Fresh Whipped Cream (*see recipe on page 164*) and your favorite berries!

CALIFORNIA DRESSING

1 lemon, juiced
¼ cup FCP extra virgin olive oil
2 tablespoons grape seed oil
¼ cup red grapes
1 teaspoon elephant garlic, shredded
1 teaspoon lecithin powder (optional)
½ teaspoon nutritional yeast flakes
½ teaspoon RealSalt

Combine all ingredients in a blender or food processor until smooth. Refrigerate until ready to use. Dressings can be made in advance. Keep refrigerated and use within 24 hours.

CALIFORNIA SALAD

    1 head butter lettuce
    1 avocado, cut up
    ½ cup cucumber, chopped
    1 tablespoon sunflower seeds
    1 tablespoon fresh chives, finely chopped
    1 Roma tomato, chopped
    ½ cup alfalfa sprouts

Wash all ingredients in water with a drop of food-grade hydrogen peroxide or filtered or bottled water. Drain lettuce on paper towels or in a salad spinner. In a large salad bowl, combine all ingredients. Keep chilled until ready to serve. Add dressing, toss well, and serve immediately.

This salad is great a la carte, or serve topped with grilled shrimp for a summer meal.

CAPRESE SALAD

    7 ounces fresh buffalo mozzarella cheese,
        sliced into ¼-inch-thick slices
    3 Roma or Heirloom tomatoes, sliced into ½-inch thick slices
    1 bunch fresh basil leaves, whole
    1 tablespoon elephant garlic, pressed
    ½ cup FCP extra virgin olive oil
    2 tablespoons balsamic vinegar
    Dash RealSalt
    Dash cayenne pepper

On a serving platter, layer tomato slices, followed by one basil leaf for each tomato slice. Place cheese slices on top of the basil. Set aside. In a food processor, combine oil, vinegar, garlic, salt, and pepper. Drizzle the dressing over the platter in a circular pattern.

This recipe is best served well chilled as an appetizer or as a salad with your favorite Italian-inspired dish.

CHACOCOBAN CAKE

2 ripe bananas, mashed
¼ cup dried coconut, shredded and unsweetened
¼ cup organic unsalted butter, softened
½ cup Sucanat
½ cup organic dark chocolate chips
1 duck egg, whisked
1 cup goat's milk
1 cup whole-wheat pastry flour
1 tablespoon baking powder
Pinch RealSalt

In a large mixing bowl combine bananas with butter. Whisk in Sucanat, egg, coconut, and chips. Add flour in half-cup increments, alternating with milk in half-cup increments; add baking powder and salt. Continue whisking until all ingredients are incorporated. Lightly oil medium cast iron skillet and add mixture. Place in preheated 375 degree oven for 30 minutes. Let cool and serve in skillet. Cut into 8 wedges. Serve with a dollop of goat's milk ice cream or whipped organic heavy cream, drizzled with organic chocolate syrup.

CHAMOMILE TEA INFUSION

4 cups natural spring water
2 teaspoons organic chamomile flowers

Bring water to a boil. Place chamomile in teapot; pour water over. Cover and steep for 15 minutes.

It is best to have a teapot with an airtight lid to contain the essential oils and their healing properties. Chamomile tea is an excellent choice for relaxation as it helps to flush out toxins and will promote sweating, especially if taken during a RealSalt bath. I use it at the first sign of feeling under the weather or just to de-stress.

Avoid using tea bags as they are usually bleached, which contaminates the tea. It is best to use loose organic teas.

CHAMOMILE/PEPPERMINT TEA INFUSION

4 cups natural spring water
1 teaspoon dried chamomile flowers
1 teaspoon dried peppermint leaves

Bring water to a boil. Place chamomile in teapot; pour water over. Cover and steep for 15 minutes.

It is best to have a teapot with an airtight lid to contain the essential oils and their healing properties. Chamomile tea is an excellent choice for relaxation as it helps to flush out toxins and will promote sweating, especially if taken during a RealSalt bath. I use it at the first sign of feeling under the weather or just to de-stress.

Avoid using tea bags as they are usually bleached, which contaminates the tea. It is best to use loose organic teas.

CHOCOLAGE

1 cup chilled Papua New Guinea Coffee
(*see recipe on page 180*)
¼ cup organic chocolate syrup
1 ounce organic heavy cream
Dash cinnamon (optional)
8 large spring water ice cubes

Combine all ingredients in blender; liquefy until smooth. Serve immediately. Get ready for the Chocolage experience: it's the marriage of chocolate and coffee in a sea of creamy goodness.

CHOCOLATE MILK

1 cup goat's milk
2 tablespoons organic chocolate syrup
¼ teaspoon vanilla extract (optional)

Pour milk into a chilled glass; add chocolate syrup and briskly whisk. For best results use a shaker.

CINNAMON KRISPIES

1 whole-wheat-flour tortilla, cut up
1 tablespoon fructose
1 teaspoon cinnamon
¼ cup safflower oil

Cut the tortilla into four strips; then cut strips in half diagonally to yield eight bite-size pieces. Mix fructose and cinnamon in a small bowl and set aside. Heat the oil in a heavy stainless-steel skillet, and fry tortilla pieces until lightly browned on each side. Use long tongs to turn pieces. Drain on paper-towel-lined plate and sprinkle with fructose cinnamon mixture. Serves 2.

CREAMY LEMON DRESSING

1 lemon, juiced
¼ cup FCP extra virgin olive oil
½ clove elephant garlic, pressed
1 teaspoon lecithin powder (non-GMO)
½ teaspoon Kal Nutritional Yeast
RealSalt and cayenne pepper to taste

Combine all ingredients in a food processor; blend until smooth. To receive the most alkalizing, antibacterial, and essential fatty acid benefits of these ingredients, use immediately. However, it can be made in advance and refrigerated up to 24 hours. This dressing is versatile and can be used on your favorite salad combination or as a sauce on your favorite fish recipe.

CRISPY BROWN RICE CEREAL

1 bowl Organic Crispy Brown Rice Cereal
1 sun-ripened banana, sliced
1 teaspoon Sucanat (optional)
½ teaspoon cinnamon (optional)
½-1 cup goat's milk

Place all ingredients in a bowl, add milk, and enjoy a quick nutritious meal!

CRUDITÉS WITH HERB DIP

1 cup broccoli florets
1 cup cauliflower florets
1 cup jicama spears
1 cup beet circles
1 cup yam circles
1 cup asparagus spears
Herb Dip (*see recipe on page 172*)

Rinse all vegetables well in a bowl with 1-3 drops food-grade hydrogen peroxide; pat dry and cut or separate into pieces. Place in a glass dish with tight-fitting lid and chill until ready to use. Place a small bowl filled with herb dip in the center of a platter surrounded with veggies, and enjoy the enzymatic infusion!

CUCUMBER, AVOCADO, AND BEET SALAD

3 Persian cucumbers, peeled and cubed
1 whole avocado, cubed
1 small beet, shredded

Rinse produce with water and 1 drop food-grade hydrogen peroxide. To cube the cucumber, slice into quarters lengthwise and chop into pieces crosswise. Place into salad bowl; add avocado and shredded beet. Toss well with Creamy Lemon Dressing (*see recipe on page 156*).

CUCUMBER SPEARS WITH LEMON JUICE

4 Persian cucumbers, peeled and quartered lengthwise
1 whole lemon, juiced
½ teaspoon RealSalt
5 fresh mint leaves or ½ teaspoon dried mint

Place spears in a glass serving dish; drizzle with lemon juice and sprinkle with RealSalt. Keep chilled until ready to serve. Garnish with mint leaves.

EGG SALAD TRIANGLES

4 cups natural spring water
3 slices sprouted barley bread
3 medium duck eggs
1 tablespoon Daisy sour cream or crème fraîche
1 tablespoon chives, finely chopped
1 teaspoon organic prepared mustard
¼ teaspoon RealSalt
¼ teaspoon turmeric
Dash cayenne pepper

In a medium saucepan, bring water to boil. Add eggs and lower heat to a simmer. Cook 20 minutes or until hardboiled. Set eggs aside to cool. Peel, slice, and place them in a mixing bowl. Add sour cream, chives, mustard, salt, turmeric, and cayenne pepper. Combine ingredients with a pastry cutter. Lightly toast bread, cut in half diagonally, and spoon egg mixture onto triangles. Garnish with capers, dried dill, and a dash of cayenne.

EGGPLANT SPAGHETTI

16 ounces organic whole-wheat or brown rice spaghetti
28-ounce can Roma tomatoes, whole, no salt added
1 medium eggplant, peeled and chopped
1 medium red onion, chopped
1 clove elephant garlic, grated or chopped
1 bunch fresh basil, chopped, or 2 tablespoons dried basil
3 tablespoons safflower oil
1 teaspoon turmeric or organic curry powder
1 teaspoon RealSalt
½ teaspoon cayenne pepper
½ cup Pecorino Romano cheese
½ cup red wine, aged seven years (optional)
½ cup FCP extra virgin olive oil

Combine onion and eggplant with oil in a large, solid stainless-steel or cast iron skillet only, place under broiler for 10 minutes or until browned, remove from broiler and set on the stove. Add basil, tomatoes, garlic, turmeric, and cayenne pepper. Add wine and bring to a boil; reduce to a simmer for 20 minutes. Remove from heat and set aside.

In a large stainless-steel pot bring 4 quarts of fresh water to a rolling boil. Carefully place the pasta in boiling water. Stir frequently to prevent sticking. Cook 10 minutes or until al dente. Remove from heat, drain, and toss with olive oil and a dash of RealSalt. Place cooked pasta in a large serving dish, pour sauce over pasta, and garnish with Pecorino Romano cheese and fresh basil leaves.

ENGLISH MUFFIN PIZZA

6 whole-wheat English muffins
2 ounces goat's Gouda cheese, grated
2 ounces Manchego cheese, grated
1 ounce Pecorino Romano cheese, grated
1 can jumbo black pitted olives, sliced
1 can artichoke hearts, sliced (packed in water)

Pizza Sauce

14 ounces organic Roma tomatoes, no salt added
½ cup safflower oil
1 tablespoon Kal Nutritional Yeast Flakes
Dash cayenne pepper
2 tablespoons All Purpose Herb Blend
1 tablespoon Red Onion Blend
1 tablespoon Elephant Garlic Blend
1 tablespoon RealSalt

- or -

½ medium red onion, chopped
1 clove elephant garlic, pressed
1 teaspoon dried oregano
1 teaspoon dried basil
1 teaspoon dried thyme
1 teaspoon RealSalt
1 teaspoon fennel, ground

Preheat oven to 400 degrees. Cut muffins in half and place them on stainless-steel cookie sheet or baking stone. Bake until muffins are lightly toasted, approximately 5 minutes. Ladle each toasted muffin with pizza sauce, then layer with Manchego and Gouda cheese blend, and garnish with black olives and artichoke hearts. Sprinkle with Pecorino Romano cheese. Bake about 5 minutes or until cheese is melted.

Additional topping suggestions: sautéed eggplant, red onion, Crimini mushrooms, elephant garlic, soft goat's cheese, feta.

ENZYMATIC SHIRAZI SALAD

8 medium Persian cucumbers or 4 regular cucumbers
4 medium Roma tomatoes
1 whole avocado, cut into pieces
½ medium red onion, chopped
1 teaspoon dried mint or 1 tablespoon fresh mint leaves,
   chopped
¼ cup FCP extra virgin olive oil
1 lemon, juiced
½ teaspoon RealSalt
1 teaspoon lecithin powder (non-GMO)
Dash cayenne pepper

Peel and chop cucumbers; combine with coarsely chopped tomatoes, onion, and avocado. Next sprinkle with mint; rub the mint between your palm and fingers to release the essential oils. In a food processor combine olive oil, lemon juice, elephant garlic, lecithin powder, and cayenne pepper until smooth. Pour dressing over salad, sprinkle with RealSalt, and toss. For best results, chill for at least 2 hours.

ENZYMATIC TABOULI

1 cup organic bulgur, cooked
1 bunch cilantro, chopped
1 bunch basil, chopped
2 stalks leek, finely sliced
2 cups kale, chopped
½ cup fresh dill, finely chopped
1 English cucumber or 5 Persian cucumbers, chopped
5 Roma tomatoes, chopped
1 large avocado or 2 small avocadoes, cubed

Dressing

2 medium lemons, juiced
¾ cup FCP extra virgin olive oil
1 teaspoon RealSalt
½ teaspoon cayenne pepper
1 teaspoon Kal Nutritional Yeast Flakes
1 teaspoon elephant garlic powder
   or 2 teaspoons elephant garlic, freshly grated
1 teaspoon lecithin powder (non-GMO)

In saucepan, boil 3 cups fresh water; add bulgur and simmer for 10 minutes. Do not overcook. Rinse with cold water, drain, and set aside. Combine lemon juice, olive oil, salt, pepper, yeast flakes, and garlic; whisk until blended. In a large glass bowl, combine bulgur, tomatoes, and dressing; toss well. Add leeks, cilantro, basil, dill, and cucumber. Use your hands to gently combine the ingredients. For best flavor, marinate this mixture overnight. Before serving add avocado and toss well.

On a large platter, arrange kale. Pour tabouli in the center of the platter, overlapping the kale; garnish with kalamata olives, cucumber slices, and tomato wedges.

living beyond organic

EZ YAM CUSTARD PIE

4 medium yams, baked
1 medium duck egg
½ cup organic heavy cream
4 tablespoons Sucanat
¼ cup Grade B maple syrup
1 teaspoon ground cinnamon
1 tablespoon vanilla extract, alcohol-free

Graham Cracker Crust

1 16-ounce box New Morning graham crackers
1 tablespoon raw almonds, ground
½ cup organic unsalted butter, softened
¼ teaspoon ground cardamom (optional)
1 teaspoon Simple Syrup (optional; *see recipe on page 197*)

Preheat oven to 375 degrees. Rinse yams, pierce with a fork, and place in glass baking dish. Top with parchment paper and cover tightly with aluminum foil. Bake 1 hour or until cooked, but firm (do not overcook). Once the yams are cool enough to touch, peel, and mash in a large mixing bowl. In a separate bowl, whisk eggs, cream, maple syrup, cinnamon, and vanilla; if a smoother consistency is preferred, use an electric mixer to blend egg mixture and yams.

Place graham crackers in a food processor to yield a medium grind. Pour the crumbs into a glass or porcelain pie pan along with ground almonds, cardamom, and butter. Use your fingers to blend ingredients together. Gently press down on bottom and sides to form crust. If mixture is too dry, add Simple Syrup. Preheat oven to 375 degrees. Pour yam mixture into unbaked crust. Bake pie 45 to 50 minutes. Test center. If knife comes out clean, the pie is done. Allow pie to cool before serving.

My daughter Tiara loves this pie with Fresh Whipped Cream (*see recipe on page 164*)!

FRESH MANGO SLICES WITH CAYENNE

1 large mango, peeled and cut
1 fresh lime, juiced
Dash RealSalt and cayenne pepper

Rinse mango in water with 1 drop food-grade hydrogen peroxide. Pat dry, score skin in quarter sections, peel back skin to reveal mango. Slice mango off of bone, place slices onto chilled plate, drizzle with lime juice, and sprinkle with RealSalt and cayenne pepper.

FRESH PINEAPPLE TRIANGLES

1 ripe pineapple, chilled
4 sprigs fresh mint, optional

Snap off green top, which can be reserved for a centerpiece. Place pineapple in a bowl of fresh water with 1 drop of food-grade hydrogen peroxide and pat dry. Cut ends off, then cut into quarters lengthwise. Slice each quarter into 1-inch triangles. Leave triangles in skin. Arrange on a platter and garnish with mint sprigs. This is a festive and easy way to serve pineapple without having to peel it!

FRESH WHIPPED CREAM

1 pint organic heavy cream
¼ cup Simple Syrup (*see recipe on page 197*)
  or Grade B maple syrup
½ teaspoon organic cornstarch
1 teaspoon vanilla extract, alcohol-free

Pour cream into electric mixer. Add cornstarch. Start whipping; slowly drizzle in syrup and vanilla. Continue whipping until cream is stiff. If you prefer, you can use a large mixing bowl and a wire whisk. Refrigerate until ready to use.

FROZEN MANGO DELIGHT

    1 large mango, peeled and cut
    12 cubes frozen almond milk
    ¼ cup organic heavy cream (optional)
    1 tablespoon Grade B maple syrup

Place mango, syrup, and 3 ice cubes in blender; add more cubes and cream until desired consistency is achieved.

FRUIT CRISP

    3 cups red Bartlett pears, cored and sliced
      (or substitute other fruit)
    ¼ cup whole-wheat pastry flour
    ¼ cup fructose
    1 tablespoon lemon juice
    1 teaspoon vanilla extract, alcohol-free
    1 ounce Absolut vodka (optional)

Combine all ingredients and toss well. Pour mixture into a glass or porcelain baking dish and set aside.

Crisp

    ¾ cup whole-wheat flour
    ¼ cup rolled barley
    ½ cup Sucanat
    1 tablespoon almonds, coarsely ground
    1 teaspoon cinnamon
    Pinch cardamom
    Pinch RealSalt
    ½ cup organic unsalted butter

Blend butter and the dry ingredients with a pastry cutter, taking care not to overwork the mixture. Once the butter is cut up, use your fingertips to crumble mixture over the fruit. Preheat oven to 375 degrees and bake for 30 minutes or until golden brown and bubbly. Try it with a dollop of crème fraîche! Crème fraîche is available in your grocer's refrigerated dairy case.

FRUITY BANANA SPLIT

1 banana, peeled and sliced lengthwise
¼ cup fresh pineapple, chopped
¼ cup fresh strawberries, hulled and chopped
1 tablespoon Grade B maple syrup or raw honey
2 tablespoons chocolate syrup
1 tablespoon Fresh Whipped Cream (*see recipe on page 164*)
1 tablespoon almonds, coarsely chopped

In a small mixing bowl, combine pineapple, strawberries, and maple syrup. Place banana in a shallow bowl, cover with fruit mixture, drizzle with chocolate syrup, and top with whipped cream. Garnish with chopped almonds.

FRUITY BISON SAUSAGE

1 pound bison, ground
1 ripe pear, finely chopped
2 teaspoons All Purpose Herb Blend
1 heaping teaspoon paprika
1 teaspoon Elephant Garlic Blend
1 teaspoon Red Onion Blend
¼ cup organic whipping cream
1 teaspoon RealSalt

Combine all ingredients in a glass or stainless-steel mixing bowl; mix well. Shape into sausage links or small patties. Cook on preheated cast iron griddle or skillet. Cook approximately 4 minutes or until evenly browned on all sides. Sooo delicious!

FRUITY CHEESE SPREAD

8 ounces goat's cheese, softened
2 tablespoons goat's milk
1 cup assorted organic dried fruit, minced
1 teaspoon lavender flowers, minced (optional)
1 teaspoon lecithin powder (non-GMO)
Dash RealSalt
Dash cayenne pepper

In a medium mixing bowl combine cheese, dried fruit, flowers, and salt and pepper to taste. Using a pastry cutter, blend thoroughly; cover and refrigerate overnight. Serve on toasted barley bread for breakfast, or for a light appetizer spread on Belgian endive leaves or on organic whole grain crackers for a tasty snack. This recipe can be refrigerated for three to seven days.

GARLIC RED POTATO MASH

    8 medium red potatoes, sliced
    1 clove elephant garlic, grated
    ¼ cup organic heavy cream
    4 tablespoons organic unsalted butter
    1 teaspoon RealSalt
    1 teaspoon fresh chives (optional)
    Dash cayenne pepper
    3 quarts fresh water

Wash potatoes thoroughly. It is best to use organic; if you are using conventional potatoes, peel them. Remove all eyes. Slice ¼- to ½-inch thick. Place potatoes in a large pot; pour just enough water to cover potatoes. Bring to a boil. Simmer for 15 minutes covered until potatoes are fork tender. Do not overcook. Remove from heat; drain water. Add butter, garlic, and cream. Mash the ingredients one at a time with a masher for a rustic texture or combine all ingredients in an electric mixer for a smooth creamy texture. Add RealSalt to taste. Garnish with fresh chives. Serve immediately.

GOOD OLD-FASHIONED POPCORN

½ cup organic popping corn
¼ cup safflower oil
Organic unsalted butter, melted to taste
RealSalt to taste

In a large deep pot with a tight-fitting lid, heat oil. Add corn; cover and slide pot back and forth over a medium flame until all of it has popped. Pour popped corn into a large serving bowl, sprinkle with RealSalt, and drizzle with melted butter, or try it with homemade caramel sauce!

Caramel Sauce

4 tablespoons organic unsalted butter
2 tablespoons Sucanat
¼ cup Grade B maple syrup
¼ cup organic heavy cream

In a small saucepan melt butter over medium heat; stir in syrup and Sucanat. Continuously stirring heat until bubbly, slowly stir cream into the mixture. Continue stirring until it thickens. Drizzle over popcorn for a satisfying treat!

GOUDA CHEESE QUESADILLA

2 medium whole-wheat-flour tortillas
4 slices goat's Gouda cheese

Heat a stainless-steel or cast iron skillet over a medium flame. Place a tortilla in the skillet, arrange cheese slices on the tortilla so that the cheese melts evenly, and cover with another tortilla. Press with a spatula and turn until cheese is melted. This is a great appetizer or after-school snack, served with guacamole, salsa, and sour cream.

GOURMET GRILLED SHRIMP

1 package fresh or frozen freshwater wild jumbo shrimp
½ cup tamari
¼ cup safflower oil
1 ounce sake or pineapple juice
1 bunch cilantro, chopped
1 tablespoon elephant garlic, grated
1 tablespoon ginger root, grated
1 organic lemon, juiced
1 teaspoon cayenne pepper

Thaw shrimp in cold water; drain and place evenly across the bottom of a glass dish deep enough to hold the marinade. In a glass mixing bowl combine tamari, oil, sake, garlic, ginger, lemon juice, and cayenne pepper. Pour marinade evenly over shrimp; sprinkle with cilantro. Marinate in refrigerator approximately 3 hours. Those who wish to experience the full flavor of this recipe should marinate overnight.

Preheat your grill. Skewer shrimp, shell on, approximately 5 to 7 shrimp per skewer. Grill shrimp over medium flame approximately 5 minutes per side or until shrimp is deep reddish/orange. Be careful not to overcook.

GREEN BEANS ALMANDINE

1 pound green beans
2 tablespoons organic unsalted butter
½ cup almonds, slivered
¼ cup natural spring water
1 teaspoon Kal Nutritional Yeast Flakes
RealSalt to taste
Dash cayenne pepper

Rinse the beans well. Remove stems and place on paper towel to absorb excess moisture. In a large skillet, add enough water to cover bottom of pan. Bring to a boil. Add green beans; cover and cook over medium flame approximately 5 minutes. Beans should look bright green and firm. Do not overcook or the beans will look dull green and limp. In a small skillet, melt butter. Add almonds and cook over medium flame until lightly browned. Add yeast and salt to taste. Place green beans in serving dish; toss with butter and almond mixture. Serve immediately.

GRILLED GOUDA SANDWICH
WITH HEIRLOOM TOMATO (OPTIONAL)

2 slices sprouted barley bread
4 thin slices goat's Gouda cheese
2 teaspoons organic unsalted butter
2 slices Heirloom or Roma tomato
Fresh or dried dill, thyme, or basil leaves for garnish (optional)
RealSalt to taste
Dash cayenne pepper

Preheat a cast iron skillet. Spread butter on bread and place butter-side down in the skillet. Arrange cheese slices on the bread. Then spread butter on a second slice and place over cheese butter-side up. Using a spatula, press down on the sandwich and flip when browned. When cheese is melted, serve immediately with tomato slices sprinkled with salt and pepper and garnished with fresh or dried herb leaves. This can be served as lunch for 1 or appetizer for 4.

GUACAMOLE FANTASTICO!

3 large ripe avocados
1 lemon, juiced
3 tablespoons FCP extra virgin olive oil
1 tablespoon fresh cilantro, finely chopped
1 teaspoon dried thyme
½ teaspoon lecithin powder
1 teaspoon elephant garlic, pressed
RealSalt and cayenne pepper to taste

Cut avocados in half and remove pits. Spoon into mixing bowl; add lemon juice, olive oil, and garlic, mashing with a pastry cutter or fork. Stir in remaining ingredients. Cover and chill at least 1 hour before serving. For a chunky texture add finely chopped red onion and/or Roma tomato. This recipe can be used as a sandwich spread or a dip for veggies.

HARD-BOILED DUCK EGG

1 duck egg
1 teaspoon goat's butter
½ English muffin, toasted
¼ cup watercress, chopped (optional)
RealSalt and cayenne pepper to taste

Place egg in a small saucepan half-filled with water. Bring water to a boil over medium flame. Reduce to simmer for 15 minutes. Remove from heat and set aside. Peel and mash egg with goat's butter. Spread egg mixture on toasted muffin and season with salt and pepper to taste. Garnish with watercress.

HERB DIP

2 cups Daisy sour cream
1 8-ounce soft goat's cheese log
¼ cup Pecorino Romano cheese (optional)
1 teaspoon each dried basil, dill, thyme, oregano, and marjoram
½ teaspoon RealSalt
½ teaspoon Kal Nutritional Yeast Flakes
½ teaspoon cayenne pepper
2 tablespoons red onion, freshly grated
¼ teaspoon elephant garlic, freshly grated
RealSalt to taste

In a glass mixing bowl, combine sour cream, cheese, dried herbs, salt, yeast flakes, and cayenne pepper; whisk until blended. Cover and chill for 2 hours or overnight for more flavor.

HERB SALAD WITH JICAMA

2 medium avocados
½ cup FCP extra virgin olive oil
¼ cup lemon juice
½ cup red onion, coarsely chopped
1 teaspoon lecithin powder (non-GMO)
½ teaspoon RealSalt
Dash cayenne pepper
4 cups organic herb salad mix
1 cup jicama, chopped

Combine all ingredients except the greens and jicama in a blender to make dressing. Blend and set aside. Place greens and jicama in a large salad bowl. Pour dressing over and serve immediately. Serves 4.

HERBED BUTTER

4 ounces organic unsalted butter
¼ teaspoon RealSalt
Dash cayenne pepper
2 teaspoons All Purpose Herb Blend, or 1 teaspoon dried basil,
    1 teaspoon dried thyme, and ½ teaspoon powdered fennel

Place ingredients in a small mixing bowl and blend with a pastry cutter. Keep refrigerated until ready to use.

HOMEMADE RED KIDNEY BEANS

3 cups organic dark red kidney beans
3 quarts natural spring water
1 tablespoon RealSalt
1 bay leaf

In a large glass dish, mix beans, salt, and enough water to submerge the beans. Let soak overnight, adding water as needed. Before cooking, discard the water and rinse beans with fresh water. In a large heavy-gauge stainless-steel pot, combine beans, water, salt, and bay leaf. Bring to a boil; lower to a simmer and cook for 1 hour.

HONEY MUSTARD DRESSING

½ cup FCP extra virgin olive oil
¼ cup raw honey
2 tablespoons lemon juice
1 teaspoon organic mustard
½ teaspoon elephant garlic, pressed
½ teaspoon lecithin powder
Dash RealSalt and cayenne pepper

Blend or whisk oil, honey, lemon juice, mustard, garlic, and lecithin powder until smooth. Add RealSalt and cayenne pepper to taste. Refrigerate until ready to use.

IRON-ROASTED SALMON

2 pounds salmon fillet, wild-caught
1 medium red onion, halved and thinly sliced
¼ cup tamari, organic low sodium
¼ cup sake unfiltered (optional)
1 tablespoon sesame oil
2 teaspoons organic unsalted butter or safflower oil
½ teaspoon dried thyme
Dash RealSalt

Rinse fillet with fresh water and cut into four equal portions. Pat dry and place in a glass dish. In a small bowl whisk together tamari, sake, sesame oil, and thyme; pour mixture over salmon. Refrigerate until ready to use. Marinate for at least 2 hours or overnight for full flavor. Broil salmon in a seasoned cast iron skillet, topped with butter and onion slices and covered with marinade, for 15 minutes or until salmon and onion are golden brown.

MANDARIN SALAD

1 head butter lettuce
¼ cup cilantro, chopped
2 tangerines, peeled and sliced
¼ cup almonds, slivered
¼ cup red flame raisins
1 tablespoon organic unsalted butter

Dressing

3 tablespoons brown rice vinegar
¼ cup grape seed oil
1 tablespoon tangerine juice
1 teaspoon elephant garlic, pressed
½ teaspoon raw honey
½ teaspoon RealSalt
Dash cayenne pepper

Thoroughly rinse and drain lettuce and cilantro, preferably in a salad spinner. Gently tear lettuce into bite-size pieces. Place lettuce and cilantro in salad bowl and refrigerate. Peel tangerines and cut into ½-inch slices; separate slices into segments and add to salad bowl. Refrigerate.

To prepare dressing, combine vinegar, oil, tangerine juice, garlic, honey, RealSalt and cayenne pepper in a cruet. Shake well. Dressing can be prepared in advance and refrigerated.

In a skillet, melt butter and sauté almonds until lightly browned, stirring in raisins. Remove from heat. Sprinkle almond/raisin mixture over lettuce, pour dressing evenly over the salad, and toss gently.

The almond-raisin mixture is prepared just before salad is served.

Salad and dressing can be prepared in advance. Refrigerate until ready to serve. Toss with almond mixture, drizzle with dressing, and voila!

MOCHA COOKIES

1 cup organic unsalted butter, softened
1 cup Sucanat
½ cup Grade B maple syrup
2 duck eggs
1 tablespoon vanilla extract, alcohol-free
2 teaspoons ground Papua New Guinea Coffee
½ teaspoon cinnamon
1½ cups organic whole-wheat flour
1 cup organic barley flour
1 teaspoon baking soda
¼ teaspoon RealSalt
2 ounces organic dark chocolate chips

In a large bowl combine butter, Sucanat, and maple syrup; mix well. In a separate bowl, whisk eggs, vanilla, coffee, and cinnamon; add to butter mixture. Stir in flour, ½ cup at a time; then add baking soda, salt, and chocolate chips. Divide cookie dough into three portions. Use plastic wrap to form each portion into rolls, and chill until dough is firm. Preheat oven to 375 degrees. Slice roll into ½-inch slices. Place on a baking stone or ungreased cookie sheet, and bake approximately 12 minutes or until golden brown.

Cookie dough recipe can be prepared in advance and kept refrigerated up to 1 week.

To store, place dough on a sheet of unbleached parchment paper, roll up, and place roll in a plastic bag. Yields 3 dozen cookies.

ORANGE ROUGHY ZESTY

1 pound orange roughy fillet
½ cup low-sodium organic tamari
1 tablespoon sesame oil
½ teaspoon dried thyme
½ teaspoon dried marjoram
½ teaspoon fennel seed
1 teaspoon elephant garlic, pressed
1 teaspoon lemon zest
2 tablespoons organic unsalted butter, cut into pieces

Place fillets in a glass baking dish. Combine tamari, sesame oil, herbs, and garlic. Pour over fillets. Sprinkle with lemon zest and top with butter pieces. Cover and refrigerate for 1 hour. Preheat broiler. Place under broiler for 10 minutes or until browned and well done.

OSEKIHAN

2 cups medium grain brown rice, cooked
1 cup red kidney beans, cooked
2 tablespoons organic unsalted butter
1 teaspoon dried thyme
1 tablespoon elephant garlic, shredded
¼ cup tamari, reduced sodium
1 ounce unfiltered sake (optional)

Melt butter in a small skillet; add thyme, garlic, tamari, and sake. In a large pot, combine rice, beans, and butter mixture.

This is the best way to use any leftover rice. For a quick recipe, canned organic red kidney beans may be substituted for fresh. This Japanese-inspired dish is a complete protein source. Enjoy it a la carte or with your favorite shrimp or fish dish.

PAN-BROILED WASABI SALMON

2 pounds fresh or frozen salmon fillet, wild-caught
½ cup tamari, organic reduced sodium
1 tablespoon wasabi for mild flavor
  or 2 tablespoons wasabi for spicy flavor
1 tablespoon elephant garlic, freshly grated
1 teaspoon dried thyme
1 tablespoon fresh lemon juice
1 ounce sake (optional)
¼ cup safflower oil
½ medium red onion, sliced
4 teaspoons organic unsalted butter

Rinse fillet and place in a 9 x 13 glass dish. Rub wasabi over salmon. In a glass cruet, combine tamari, garlic, thyme, lemon juice, and sake; shake well. Spread mixture evenly over fillet; cover with a sheet of unbleached parchment paper followed by plastic wrap and refrigerate overnight.

Preheat oven to broil. Coat the bottom of a large cast iron skillet with oil. Cut the fillet into 4 equal portions and place them in the skillet. Distribute the marinade over the salmon and cover with onion slices and butter. Place skillet under broiler for approximately 15 minutes or until fillets and onion are sizzling brown. For a dramatic presentation serve salmon straight out of the broiler in the sizzling pan. This dish is excellent served with brown basmati rice. Serves 4.

PAPAYA SMOOTHIE

1 cup Meridol papaya, cut pieces
1 cup goat's milk
½ cup goat's yogurt
  or 1 capsule acidophilus/bifidus from goat's milk
2 tablespoons Grade B maple syrup
1 teaspoon non-GMO lecithin powder
3 fresh ice cubes

Place ingredients in blender for 1 minute or until smooth. This is a meal in a glass. Drink immediately.

RICH IN VITAMIN A
| and OMEGA 3 |

PAPUA NEW GUINEA COFFEE

8 cups natural spring water
½ cup Papua New Guinea Coffee, ground

Optional

½ cup organic heavy cream
½ cup Sucanat

Bring water to a boil. Place ground coffee in an 8-cup French press glass or stainless-steel beaker. Warning: beaker will be very hot. Pour 1 cup of water over coffee; swirl beaker, do not stir, so that the coffee is mixed in. Cover with lid/plunger. Brew 4 minutes. Press down gently and slowly. If there is resistance, the coffee is not settled; wait an extra minute. Once you have pressed the coffee, it is best served immediately. If you wish to use the coffee later, store in a stainless-steel container or refrigerate in a glass container with a tight-fitting lid to maintain freshness. Whether you prefer it black or with cream and sugar, this is the best full-flavored coffee ever!

Coffee can be chilled and used for café glace or Chocolage (*see recipe on page 155*).

Serve with organic heavy cream and Sucanat. For a special treat, try whipped cream with a dash of cinnamon!

PEARS WITH CHOCOLATE SAUCE

2 firm pears, cored and quartered
1 cup organic heavy cream
1 tablespoon organic unsalted butter
12 ounces organic chocolate chips
1 teaspoon vanilla extract, alcohol-free
1 teaspoon lecithin powder
1 capsule vitamin E oil (optional)

Melt butter in a medium saucepan. Stir in cream and chocolate chips. Continue stirring until chips are melted; add vanilla. Remove from heat; add lecithin powder and vitamin E. Pour some sauce in the center of a plate, arrange pears like flower petals surrounding the sauce, then drizzle choco-late sauce on top of pears. Garnish with fresh mint leaves. For an extra-rich dessert, add whipped cream or homemade vanilla ice cream.

PINEAPPLE SODA

    4 ounces pineapple juice
    3 ounces San Pelligrino sparkling mineral water
    1 ounce Grade B maple syrup
    1 ounce organic heavy cream

In a glass pitcher combine juice, sparkling mineral water and maple syrup. Stir well and pour over ice in a tall glass and top with cream.

PINEAPPLE UPSIDE-DOWN CAKE

    1½ cups whole-wheat pastry flour
    ½ cup barley flour
    1 cup Sucanat
    2 duck eggs
    ¾ cup raw almond milk
    1 teaspoon baking powder, alum-free
    1 teaspoon vanilla extract, alcohol-free
    1 teaspoon cinnamon, ground

Preheat oven to 375 degrees. Combine flours, Sucanat, eggs, almond milk, baking powder, vanilla, and cinnamon. Mix well. Keep chilled until ready to use. Prepare baking pan. You can use a 9 x 13 glass or stainless-steel pan, but I prefer baking in a cast iron skillet.

    1 tablespoon safflower oil to coat pan
    2 cups fresh pineapple, chopped
    3 tablespoons organic unsalted butter or coconut butter
    ½ cup Sucanat
    1 teaspoon vanilla extract, alcohol-free

(*continued on page 182*)

PINEAPPLE UPSIDE-DOWN CAKE (continued)

Pour the oil into baking pan, coating bottom and sides. In a medium saucepan, melt butter over a medium-low flame. Add pineapple, Sucanat, and vanilla. Stir until Sucanat is dissolved. Pour mixture into baking pan, followed by cake mixture. Bake 45 minutes or until cake is done. Cool. Run a knife along the edges to loosen cake. Place a serving dish over the cake and flip it over. If some of the cake sticks to the bottom of the pan, use a spatula to lift it out and place the pieces onto cake. Don't worry. Once you dress it up with a dollop of fresh whipped cream, no one will notice.

PINEAPPLE WITH HONEY YOGURT SAUCE

1 pineapple
1 cup goat's yogurt
¼ cup honey, raw
1 teaspoon lemon juice
Dash cayenne pepper

Tear off the top of a chilled pineapple and slice off both ends. Quarter the pineapple lengthwise; slice core off the tops of each quarter. Start where the skin meets the pineapple and cut across to remove skin. Cut pineapple into bite-size pieces. Place in a glass serving dish and refrigerate until ready to serve. For sauce, combine all other ingredients in a bowl and whisk until creamy. Pour sauce over pineapple and garnish with fresh mint leaves.

Note: You may use this yogurt sauce in other recipes simply by omitting the pineapple.

PINK PEAR PIE

2 Basic Piecrusts (*see recipe on page 134*)
7 red Bartlett pears, cored, halved, and sliced
1 tablespoon whole-wheat pastry flour
¼ cup fructose

1 tablespoon beet powder
1 teaspoon cinnamon
1 teaspoon vanilla extract, alcohol-free
1 tablespoon vodka (optional)
¼ cup organic heavy cream

Place pear slices in a large mixing bowl. Add cream, vanilla, and vodka; toss well and set aside. In a separate bowl, mix flour, beet powder, fructose, and cinnamon. Combine powder mixture with pear mixture.

Prepare crust in a glass or porcelain pie pan, press evenly on the bottom and sides. Pour pear filling into piecrust. Roll out crust and cut strips, arrange strips on top of filling to form a lattice pattern, or cover pie with whole crust and put small slices in top to release air and moisture. Pinch edges together to secure strips.

Bake for 15 minutes in an oven preheated to 400 degrees, and then lower the setting to 375 degrees and bake for 30 minutes or until top is golden brown.

PITA POCKET SANDWICH

½ whole-wheat pita
½ avocado, sliced
2 fresh basil leaves, chopped
½ cup alfalfa sprouts
2 tablespoons Seasoned Olive Oil (see below)

Fill ingredients into pita pocket and drizzle with olive oil.

Seasoned Olive Oil

1 cup FCP extra virgin olive oil
½ teaspoon RealSalt
¼ teaspoon cayenne pepper
1 teaspoon dried oregano
1 teaspoon lecithin powder (non-GMO)

Whisk all ingredients together in a bowl. Refrigerate in a glass cruet. Shake well before each use.

POMMES A LA CHRISTARA
(RED POTATOES WITH LAVENDER)

    4 medium red potatoes, cubed
    ¼ cup safflower oil
    5 lavender blossoms and leaves, finely chopped
    2 tablespoons organic unsalted butter
    ½ teaspoon RealSalt
    ¼ teaspoon cinnamon
    1 tablespoon honey

Preheat large cast iron skillet. Add oil and potatoes; cook evenly until golden brown. Use a spatula to turn as they brown. Add butter and salt to enhance the browning. For a unique flavor, add lavender blossoms and leaves during last 5 minutes of cooking. Sprinkle with cinnamon and drizzle with honey.

QUICK-FRIED BEANS

    2 cans organic red kidney beans, rinsed
    1 teaspoon dried thyme
    2 tablespoons organic heavy cream
    1 teaspoon RealSalt
    1 teaspoon freshly grated elephant garlic
    Dash cayenne pepper
    2 tablespoons safflower oil

Drain beans and place in a glass mixing bowl. Rinse with fresh clean water. Sprinkle with RealSalt, using your hands to mix well. Heat oil in a heavy stainless-steel skillet; combine beans, cream, herbs, and spices; mash until creamy. Remove from heat and set aside.

Heat a large cast iron skillet over a medium flame. Place whole-wheat-flour tortilla in skillet; heat about 30 seconds per side. Fill with beans, meat, guacamole, and salsa; garnish with sour cream and fresh cilantro.

QUICK FRIES

6 medium red potatoes
1 teaspoon dried thyme
1 teaspoon dried basil
1 teaspoon dried oregano
½ cup safflower oil

Scrub and rinse potatoes well. Drain and pat dry with paper towels; remove any eyes. Cut in half lengthwise, place flat side down, cut into ¼-inch slices, and place in a large mixing bowl. Combine with thyme, basil, oregano, and oil. Use your hands to thoroughly coat potatoes with oil mix. Spread coated potatoes on a large stainless-steel baking pan (minimum 1-inch deep) to hold oil. Place under broiler for 10 minutes or until browned; then turn and repeat until potatoes are evenly browned and crispy—about 20 minutes total. Sprinkle with RealSalt to taste.

QUICK SANDWICH SPREAD

¼ cup Daisy sour cream
1 teaspoon organic mustard
Pinch of dried or fresh thyme (optional)
Dash RealSalt and cayenne pepper

Combine all ingredients in a small glass bowl and mix well.

QUICK STRAWBERRY SORBET

1 teaspoon lemon rind, finely grated
½ cup Simple Syrup (*see recipe on page 197*)
  or Grade B maple syrup
1 teaspoon lemon juice
3 cups frozen strawberries
1 teaspoon lecithin powder (non-GMO)

Combine all ingredients in a blender. Use immediately or pour mixture into a glass storage container with a tight-fitting lid; store in the freezer until ready to use. This makes about a quart.

RAW ALMOND MILK

1 pound raw almonds
3 cups natural spring water
½ teaspoon vanilla extract, alcohol-free
1 date (optional)
3 cups natural spring water

living beyond organic

Place almonds in a glass bowl; submerge in 3 cups water and cover tightly. Place the bowl in the refrigerator overnight. Drain and discard the water; place the almonds, vanilla extract, and date in a blender with 3 cups of fresh water and liquefy. Strain mixture into a glass container. Cover and refrigerate. Use within 48 hours. Save the pulp for Almond Spice Muffins (*see recipe on page 126*). The less water you use when liquefying, the creamier the milk will be.

RAW SOAKED ALMONDS

1 cup raw almonds
2 cups natural spring water

Place almonds in a glass bowl or jar with tight-fitting lid. Pour water over the almonds; cover and refrigerate overnight. The almonds will absorb water and be easy to peel. Serve yourself in half-cup servings. Peel and enjoy!

This is a great anytime snack, high in protein and vitamin E. The almonds are easier to digest when peeled because you are eliminating the enzyme inhibitors.

RED BEAN BURRITO

1 can organic red kidney beans, rinsed or
   Homemade Red Kidney Beans (*see recipe on page 173*)
1 ounce organic heavy cream
2 tablespoons safflower oil
1 teaspoon RealSalt
1 teaspoon dried thyme
Dash cayenne pepper
4 Ezekiel or organic whole-wheat-flour tortillas
1 cup goat's Gouda cheese grated (optional)

Heat oil in skillet; add beans, cream, thyme, salt, and pepper. Mash ingredients until smooth. Remove from heat. In a hot cast iron skillet warm tortilla on both sides. Spoon bean mixture into tortilla; sprinkle with cheese. Fold both ends, and roll them up lengthwise. Makes 4 burritos.

RED ENCHILADAS

    3 ounces dried red Anaheim chili pods
    1 clove elephant garlic, pressed
    1 cup fresh cilantro leaves
    ½ cup red onion, chopped
    1 teaspoon dried oregano
    1 teaspoon RealSalt
    1 teaspoon red wine vinegar
    ¼ cup safflower oil
    ¼ teaspoon cayenne pepper (optional)
    1 Roma tomato (optional)
    2 cups goat's Gouda cheese, shredded
    1 cup sheep's milk Manchego cheese, shredded
    1 dozen organic corn tortillas

In a medium saucepan bring 2 cups fresh water to boil, add chili pods, simmer for 15 minutes until pods are tender. Remove from heat, reserving ¼ cup of water. Hold chili pods with tongs, pull off stems, and discard. Place chili pods in blender; add oil, garlic, onion, tomato, and salt; liquefy until smooth. Set aside. Set up an assembly line: tortillas, skillet with hot oil, chili sauce in a round pan, shredded cheese, sliced olives, cilantro leaves, and a rectangular baking dish. Place a tortilla in hot oil approximately 10 seconds on each side; dip both sides in chili mixture; place in bake ware; and fill with cheese, olives, and cilantro. Roll tortilla, place fold-side down, and slide to the edge. Continue until all tortillas are filled and lined up in bake ware; layer if necessary. Garnish with chili sauce, cheese, and chives. Bake in a preheated 375-degree oven for 20 minutes, the last 5 minutes uncovered. Garnish with sliced olives, fresh chives, and a dollop of sour cream if desired. If the chili is too sweet, add cayenne pepper; if too spicy, add Roma tomato.

RED LENTIL SOUP

1 cup red lentils
4 cups natural spring water
½ cup red onion, chopped
½ cup leek, thinly sliced
2 tablespoons safflower oil
1 medium red potato, grated
1 teaspoon RealSalt
1 teaspoon turmeric
1 tablespoon non-GMO lecithin powder
Dash cayenne pepper

In a medium saucepan, heat oil over medium flame. Add onion and leek; cook for 5 minutes, stirring until lightly browned. Add lentils, turmeric, and water. Bring to a boil. Add potato. Reduce heat and simmer for 25 minutes or until lentils are tender. To thicken soup, add lecithin powder. Ladle soup into bowls, drizzle with olive oil and/or heavy cream, and garnish with fresh cilantro leaves. Yummy! For those who prefer lighter fare, garnish with a lemon slice, or for a creamy texture, try a dollop of crème fraîche.

RED POTATO FLOWER SALAD

2 small organic red potatoes, thinly sliced
1 cup Guacamole Fantastico! (*see recipe on page 171*)
RealSalt and cayenne to taste
Garnish with alfalfa sprouts or edible flowers (optional)

Start with well chilled red potatoes, sliced thin. On a salad plate arrange potato slices in a circular pattern, overlapping like flower petals; sprinkle with salt. Leave a space in the center, and fill with guacamole. Garnish with edible flowers or fresh cilantro. This dish is very alkalizing, provides oleic and lipoic fatty acids to help detox rancid fat and is an incredible enzyme boost that will aid in digestion and improve regularity.

Note: Always wash potatoes in water with 1-2 drops of food-grade hydrogen peroxide, and cut out any enzyme inhibitors (roots or eyes).

RED POTATO LEEK SOUP

4 red potatoes, sliced
4 cups natural spring water
1 cup leek, chopped
1 tablespoon organic unsalted butter
1 cup goat's milk
1 teaspoon RealSalt
1 teaspoon dried thyme
1 tablespoon lecithin powder (non-GMO)
Dash cayenne pepper
¼ cup organic heavy cream (optional)

Melt butter in a medium saucepan. Add leek and cook for 2 minutes. Add potatoes and cook for an additional minute; stir in thyme, salt, and water. Bring to a boil. Reduce heat and simmer for 20 minutes or until potatoes are tender. Remove from heat, drain and save potato liquid, and mash potatoes in pot. Over low flame stir in milk, add lecithin powder and saved water, and stir until soup thickens. Add cayenne pepper to taste. Straining and blending solids provides a creamy texture. Serve immediately garnished with fresh thyme.

RED RICE WITH BISON

4 cups brown basmati rice
6 cups natural spring water
1 28-ounce can whole Roma tomatoes, chopped
2 pounds marinated bison top sirloin, in 1- to 2-inch pieces
1 cup red onion, chopped
1 teaspoon turmeric
½ teaspoon cinnamon
1 tablespoon RealSalt
1 tablespoon marjoram
½ teaspoon cayenne pepper
¼ cup red wine or red wine vinegar
½ cup safflower oil
1 teaspoon dried thyme
2 whole red potatoes sliced

To prepare meat

Trim excess fat and membrane, cut sirloin into bite size pieces. In a large pot, heat half of the oil over medium flame. Add meat pieces and ½ cup onion; sauté 5 minutes. Next, add enough water to cover mixture (approx. 2 cups). Cover and bring to a boil; reduce heat and simmer for 1 hour or until meat is fork tender. You can use a pressure cooker to reduce cooking time. While meat is cooking you can start the rice.

When meat is done add the following ingredients into the pot of cooked meat: Roma tomatoes (with juice), turmeric, salt, marjoram, cayenne, and red wine vinegar. Bring to a boil; reduce heat and simmer for 20 minutes. Set aside until rice is ready.

To prepare rice

In a large pot, heat remaining oil; add remaining onion, rice, thyme, salt, and 6 cups fresh water. Cover and bring to a boil over medium flame; reduce heat and simmer for 25 minutes. Rice will be par cooked. Keep covered and set aside.

When meat sauce is done, gently fold it into the cooked rice until rice is evenly coated with meat sauce.

In a large deep skillet, over a medium flame heat ¼ cup of oil, line with sliced potatoes, and pour rice mixture into skillet over potatoes. Cover and simmer for 15 minutes or until potatoes are nicely browned.

To serve

Transfer rice onto serving platter. Slide spatula under potatoes and garnish rice with them, brown-side up.

Recommendations

This dish is best served as an entree, with Enzymatic Shirazi Salad (*see recipe on page 161*) and goat's yogurt on the side. A meal sure to please the entire family!

SALAD-STUFFED WHOLE-WHEAT PITA WITH CREAMY LEMON DRESSING

½ cup FCP extra virgin olive oil
¼ cup lemon juice
½ teaspoon elephant garlic, pressed
1 teaspoon lecithin powder
½ teaspoon fennel powder
¼ teaspoon dried thyme, ground
½ teaspoon RealSalt
Dash cayenne pepper
1 whole-wheat pita, cut in half
½ cup alfalfa sprouts
1 cup baby mixed greens, chopped
1 Roma tomato, chopped
1 duck egg, boiled (optional)

Place oil, lemon juice, garlic, lecithin powder, fennel powder, thyme, RealSalt, and cayenne pepper in blender or whisk briskly in a bowl. Refrigerate until ready to use. Rinse greens in filtered water with 1 drop food-grade hydrogen peroxide and spin or pat dry with paper towels. Place in a large salad bowl. Toss with some of the dressing, and then stuff salad mixture into pita halves. Slice egg and arrange equal portions in each pita. Drizzle the remaining dressing into the pita (*see recipe on page 156*).

SALMON PONZU

1½ pounds wild-caught salmon fillet
½ cup tamari
¼ cup fresh organic lemon juice
1 ounce natural spring water
1 ounce sake
1 teaspoon dried thyme
1 teaspoon fresh ginger, grated
1 teaspoon fresh elephant garlic, grated
1 teaspoon roasted sesame seeds
1 tablespoon fresh chives, chopped
½ teaspoon cayenne pepper
3 tablespoons organic unsalted butter
RealSalt to taste

Rinse salmon; pat dry; and sprinkle with RealSalt, sesame seeds, and thyme. Place in a glass baking dish, top with bits of butter, and keep refrigerated until ready to use.

Ponzu Sauce

In a mixing bowl combine tamari, lemon juice, sake, ginger, garlic, chives, and cayenne. Whisk together until blended. This recipe can be made in advance and chilled until ready to use.

To cook

Preheat broiler. Place salmon in a cast iron skillet, pour half of the Ponzu sauce over salmon, and broil for 15 minutes or until golden brown.

Serve immediately with reserved Ponzu sauce for dipping. This dish is excellent as a hot appetizer a la carte or as a main course served with noodles or brown rice.

SALMON SALAD SANDWICH
(SUPER ALTERNATIVE TO TUNA)

1 can wild-caught salmon or 1 cup left-over salmon

¼ cup fennel bulb, chopped

¼ cup red onion, finely chopped

1 tablespoon fresh thyme or basil, chopped,
    or 1 teaspoon dried thyme or basil

2 tablespoons Daisy sour cream

1 teaspoon horseradish, grated

½ teaspoon turmeric

½ teaspoon RealSalt

Dash cayenne pepper

Combine all ingredients in a glass mixing bowl. Mash well to yield a smooth consistency. Keep refrigerated until ready to serve. This recipe can be made in advance.

To assemble sandwich

2 slices sprouted barley bread, lightly toasted

2 tablespoons salmon salad

1 leaf butter lettuce

2 slices Roma tomato

1 tablespoon organic mustard (optional)

Start with a generous helping of salmon salad and then layer the rest of the ingredients as desired. Cut sandwich in half diagonally and enjoy!

SAVORY BROWN RICE

2 cups brown basmati rice

3 cups filtered or natural spring water

2 tablespoons safflower oil

1 tablespoon All Purpose Herb Blend
or combine thyme, marjoram, and ground fennel

1 teaspoon Onion Blend
or ½ cup red onion, chopped and sautéed

1 tablespoon organic unsalted butter, cut in pieces
(or grape seed oil for drizzling)

RealSalt to taste

In large stainless-steel pot, heat oil over medium flame. Add onion and sauté until lightly browned. Add rice, thyme. Gently pour the water into pot over rice mixture. Over high flame bring to a boil. Reduce flame to low. Cover and simmer for approximately 30 minutes. Turn off flame and allow the rice to rest. Meanwhile, melt butter, add salt, and stir. Drizzle over rice and serve. Or combine salt with grape seed oil for additional antioxidant benefits.

SCRUMPTIOUS FRENCH TOAST

3 slices sprouted barley bead
1 duck egg
½ cup goat's milk
½ teaspoon cinnamon, ground
½ teaspoon vanilla extract, alcohol-free
½ teaspoon almond extract (optional)
2 biscuits Weetabix, crumbled
2 tablespoons organic unsalted butter
1 tablespoon dark chocolate, coarsely grated
¼ cup Grade B maple syrup

In a mixing bowl, whisk eggs, milk, cinnamon, vanilla, and almond extract until smooth. In a separate bowl crumble Weetabix. Melt butter in a large skillet. Slice bread on the diagonal, dip into egg batter, and dredge in Weetabix. Gently place into hot skillet and brown on each side until done, approximately 1 minute per side. Drizzle with maple syrup or chocolate syrup as desired and serve.

Weetabix can be substituted with crispy brown rice (Koala Crisp), or for a nutty flavor use fresh ground almonds.

SCRUMPTIOUS HASH BROWNS (FOR CHILI AND LACE)

¼ cup safflower oil
2 medium red potatoes, coarsely grated
½ teaspoon dried thyme
RealSalt to taste after cooking

In large skillet, heat oil over medium flame. Add potatoes to cover bottom of skillet, sprinkle with thyme and salt. With a spatula, turn potatoes when brown. Continue cooking until browned evenly on both sides. Drain on paper towels. Serve immediately. Use RealSalt to taste after cooking.

This recipe is an excellent choice for breakfast, served with fresh papaya and a cup of Papua New Guinea Coffee (*see recipe on page 180*) with cream and Sucanat (optional) or herb tea.

SEVEN VEGGIE SOBA

1 8-ounce package soba noodles
8 cups natural spring water
1 beet, juliennes
1 crookneck squash, chopped
½ cup fennel bulb, chopped
½ cup yam, chopped
½ cup red onion, coarsely chopped
¾ cup kale, shredded
1 cup mung bean sprouts (optional)
1 tablespoon ginger, freshly grated
1 tablespoon elephant garlic, grated
¼ cup toasted sesame seed oil
¼ cup organic tamari or Bragg Liquid Aminos
2 tablespoons toasted sesame seeds (optional)
¼ teaspoon cayenne pepper

Fill a 4 quart pot halfway with water; bring to a boil. Add soba and boil for 10 minutes or until fork tender. In a wok or large skillet, heat sesame oil and lightly stir-fry veggies starting with the onions and fennel first, then all the rest (reserve the kale). Add tamari and cayenne to veggies as they cook. Drain noodles, place in a large mixing bowl, and add veggie stir-fry. Mix well and toss kale in at the last minute so that it wilts with the heat of the cooked noodles. Garnish with sesame seeds and serve immediately.

This recipe is great chilled as a pasta salad. For variety, add or substitute the vegetables with organic edamame, broccoli, cauliflower, or eggplant.

SIMPLE DRESSING

¼ cup red wine vinegar or lemon juice
½ cup FCP extra virgin olive oil
1 teaspoon All Purpose Herb Blend

– or –

1 teaspoon elephant garlic, pressed
¼ teaspoon dried thyme
½ teaspoon RealSalt
Dash cayenne pepper

Place ingredients in a blender for 30 seconds or whisk to-gether. This dressing is simple, time saving, and provides antioxidants and antibacterial properties. It's the perfect background for all your fresh organic produce. Try substi-tuting the vinegar with lemon juice for alkalizing benefits and a vitamin C infusion.

SIMPLE SCRAMBLE

1 duck egg
1 tablespoon organic heavy cream or 1 tablespoon goat's milk
Dash RealSalt
Dash cayenne pepper
1 teaspoon organic unsalted butter

Combine egg, cream, salt, and pepper in a small bowl and whisk until smooth. Melt butter in a small skillet; pour in egg mixture. Allow to cook for 1 minute and scramble. Serve with a slice of buttered toast, cut in half.

SIMPLE SYRUP

½ cup Sucanat
1 teaspoon vanilla extract, alcohol-free
2 tablespoons water or Absolut vodka

Place water and vanilla in a small saucepan. Add Sucanat and stir over medium flame until Sucanat is dissolved; bring to a boil, and lower to a simmer. Continue stirring over medium flame until it starts to thicken. This recipe can be made in advance and stored in a glass container with tight-fitting lid.

SPANISH RICE

  2 cups brown rice
  1 medium red onion, chopped
  1 clove elephant garlic, pressed
  1 teaspoon dried oregano
  1 teaspoon organic chili powder
  2 Roma tomatoes, chopped
  ½ cup safflower oil
  ½ cup cilantro, chopped
  ¼ cup FCP extra virgin olive oil
  1 teaspoon RealSalt
  1 teaspoon lecithin powder (non-GMO)

In a large pot heat the oil. Add onion and cook until lightly browned. Stir in rice. Keep stirring until rice is lightly toasted. Add garlic, tomato, herbs, and spices. Gently pour in water and bring to a boil. Lower to simmer and cook for 30 minutes or until rice is tender and water is evaporated. Spoon rice onto serving dish, drizzle with salted olive oil. Garnish with cilantro.

SPICY LEMONADE

  1 large lemon
  1 tablespoon Grade B maple syrup
  Dash cayenne pepper
  8 ounces natural spring water

In a glass combine all ingredients. Add water and stir. If you choose to add ice, be sure it was made with clean water (not tap water). Or make the recipe with chilled water. This is a tasty way to help your body flush out toxins. Lemon alkalizes, Grade B maple syrup contains minerals, and cayenne pepper has antibacterial properties and stimulates circulation. You can adjust the amounts to suit your taste. I like to start my day with a glass of it. This is also known as the "Master Cleanse."

SPICY MANGO SALSA

1 mango, peeled and chopped (optional)
3 Roma tomatoes, chopped
¼ cup red onion, finely chopped
1 teaspoon elephant garlic, grated
¼ cup cilantro, finely chopped
1 whole roasted Anaheim pepper, chopped (optional)
¼ cup FCP extra virgin olive oil
1 tablespoon lemon juice
½ teaspoon RealSalt
½ teaspoon cayenne pepper

Combine all ingredients in a medium mixing bowl, mix well and chill.

This recipe can be made in advance for full flavor. Keep refrigerated up to 2 days. Serve chilled.

SPINACH SALAD WITH CRIMINI MUSHROOMS

6-8 ounces baby spinach
12 Crimini mushrooms sliced (optional)
1 small red onion, sliced and halved
1 large avocado
½ cup alfalfa sprouts

Rinse spinach in fresh water with 1 drop food-grade hydrogen peroxide. Place in salad spinner or drain on paper towels. Repeat process with mushrooms and sprouts. In large salad bowl combine spinach, mushrooms, onion, avocado, and sprouts. Toss with dressing when ready to serve.

Dressing

½ cup FCP extra virgin olive oil
¼ cup fresh lemon juice
1 tablespoon organic mustard
1 tablespoon raw pine nuts
¼ teaspoon elephant garlic, grated
1 teaspoon lecithin powder (non-GMO)
RealSalt and cayenne pepper to taste

Combine all ingredients in a blender, and blend until smooth. This recipe can be made in advance and chilled until ready to use. Store in a glass bottle or jar with a tight-fitting lid. Serves 4.

SPROUTED CORN CHIPS

1 dozen organic corn tortillas
½ cup safflower oil
½ to 1 whole teaspoon RealSalt

Cut tortillas into desired shape: strips, triangles or circles. Preheat a large skillet with ½ cup safflower oil. Cover skillet with a layer of tortilla pieces and fry until crisp, but not brown. Use cooking tongs to turn the chips. Drain on a clean paper towel, sprinkle with RealSalt. Your friends will taste the difference. One dozen organic corn tortillas yield about 72 chips. One serving equals 10 chips.

STEAMED BROCCOLI WITH LEMON ZEST

4 crowns broccoli
½ cup natural spring water
¼ cup organic grape seed oil
½ teaspoon lecithin powder (non-GMO)
Lemon zest to taste (optional)
4 lemon wedges
RealSalt and cayenne pepper to taste

Rinse broccoli well in filtered water to which you have added 1 drop food-grade hydrogen peroxide. Snap broccoli into individual florets, keeping about 1-2 inches of stem intact. Pour water into a medium stainless-steel skillet and heat over medium flame. When the water begins to boil, add broccoli. Cook for 5 minutes or until broccoli turns bright green and is still crunchy. Remove from heat and drain excess water. In a glass measuring cup, combine oil with zest, RealSalt, cayenne, and lecithin powder and whisk. Place broccoli on serving dish and drizzle with the seasoned oil. Garnish with lemon wedges. Enjoy!

This veggie dish is simple, highly nutritious, and very versatile. Try it tossed with soba as a meal. Delicious!

STUFFED AVOCADO

½ medium avocado
1 tablespoon feta cheese, crumbled
1 small Roma tomato, chopped
2 tablespoons FCP extra virgin olive oil
RealSalt and cayenne pepper to taste

Cut avocado in half lengthwise; remove pit and set aside. Refrigerate the other half. In a bowl combine feta, tomato, oil, salt, and pepper; mix well and then spoon mixture onto the avocado half.

STUFFED ROMA OR HEIRLOOM TOMATO

1 tomato
2 tablespoons Fruity Cheese Spread (*see recipe on page 166*)
Dash of All Purpose Herb Blend
Garnish with finely chopped fresh thyme or mint

Cut tomato in half, scoop out some of the middle, and mix with cheese spread. Stuff the tomato halves with cheese mixture and garnish with fresh thyme, chopped mint, or All Purpose Herb Blend. This can be made in advance and chilled.

SUNSHINE IN A SLICE

1 slice sprouted barley bread
2 tablespoons organic unsalted butter
½ Roma tomato, chopped
1 duck egg
½ teaspoon All Purpose Herb Blend
½ teaspoon Red Onion Blend
- or -
1 slice red onion, chopped
½ teaspoon dried or fresh thyme
RealSalt to taste
Dash cayenne pepper

Cut a hole in the center of the bread large enough to pour the egg inside. Set aside. Crack the egg into a glass measuring cup and set aside. Preheat skillet over medium flame. Melt 1 tablespoon butter. Add onion and cook until lightly browned. Add tomato, thyme, salt, and pepper and continue cooking until all ingredients are integrated. (If using Herb Blend and Red Onion Blend, sauté tomato instead of onion and sprinkle with seasonings.) Remove mixture from skillet and set aside. Place bread slice and hole separately in skillet. Brown and turn over. Pour egg into the slice and cook until lightly browned. Do not overcook. Gently slide a spatula under the slice and flip over. Continue cooking until done, approximately 1 minute. The egg is done when all the egg white is cooked, leaving the egg yolk soft and liquid. Remove from heat immediately. Serve your Sunshine in a Slice on a plate, ladle with tomato and onion mixture, and garnish with the sautéed hole and a sprig of fresh thyme.

SUPER PANCAKES

1 cup whole-wheat pastry flour
¼ cup barley flour (optional)
1 tablespoon milled flaxseed
½ teaspoon vanilla extract, alcohol-free (optional)
¼ teaspoon RealSalt
½ teaspoon baking powder
½ teaspoon baking soda
2 tablespoons raw wild honey
1 medium duck egg
2 cups goat's milk
2 tablespoons safflower oil
Dash cinnamon, ground

In a large mixing bowl combine the dry ingredients. In a medium mixing bowl whisk liquid ingredients; pour into dry mixture. Whisk briskly until smooth. Preheat cast iron griddle or large stainless skillet. A drop of water will bounce and sputter when the griddle is ready. Pour batter into large or small cakes; cook about 1 minute per side and check for desired browning. Serve piping hot with butter and Grade B maple syrup. Makes about 1 dozen 5-inch cakes. Absolutely amazing served with bison breakfast sausage.

SUPER PONZU

4 ounces organic low sodium tamari
1 ounce lemon juice
1 ounce lime juice
1 teaspoon sake (optional)
½ teaspoon elephant garlic, grated
¼ teaspoon ginger, grated
Dash cayenne pepper

Combine all ingredients in a glass bottle with tight-fitting lid. Cover and shake until blended. Refrigerate until ready to use. This recipe can be made in advance; it is best when chilled. Excellent as a dipping sauce or marinade for fish and bison.

SUPER TARTAR SAUCE

8 ounces crème fraîche
3 whole Bubbies Pickles, finely chopped
1 teaspoon Coleman's Dry Mustard
  or 1 teaspoon organic prepared mustard
Dash cayenne pepper
1 teaspoon lemon juice
1 teaspoon dried dill

In a mixing bowl combine crème fraîche, pickles, mustard, and dill. Whisk together, and chill. This sauce can be prepared in advance. It is a delicious accompaniment to salmon and orange roughy.

TANGERINES WITH HONEY YOGURT SAUCE

4 large honey tangerines, cut bite size
½ cup Honey Yogurt Sauce (*see recipe on page 182*)

With a sharp knife cut off ends of the tangerines, and then cut the tangerines in half. Cut skin away from the fruit to form a small tangerine-skin cup. Cut up the fruit and place it into the cup; drizzle the yogurt sauce on top. This should be served chilled. For variety try pineapple with this sushi bar-inspired dessert.

TE DE CANELLA (CINNAMON STICK TEA)

3 cups natural spring water
3 cinnamon sticks

Bring water to a boil and add cinnamon sticks. Re-boil and simmer for 2 minutes covered. Steep for 3 minutes and then serve with goat's milk and Sucanat to taste.

THYME TEA INFUSION

4 cups natural spring water
2 teaspoons thyme leaves

Bring water to boil. Place thyme in teapot. Pour boiled water over thyme; cover and steep for 10 minutes.

Thyme is one of nature's strongest antiseptic agents. It helps to relieve allergy symptoms and helps to break a fever. Tea can also be absorbed through the skin in a bath. Thyme can be combined with other herbs to make an herbal blend. Try thyme combined with peppermint for a refreshing digestive aid.

Note: Since mint and thyme are both leaves, they can be brewed together.

TOASTED ELEPHANT BREAD

1 whole organic baguette
4 ounces organic unsalted butter
1 tablespoon Pecorino Romano cheese, grated
2 teaspoons All Purpose Herb Blend

- or -

1 tablespoon elephant garlic, pressed
½ teaspoon dried thyme
½ teaspoon dried basil
½ teaspoon RealSalt
Dash cayenne pepper

In a mixing bowl combine butter with garlic, using a pastry cutter. Add All Purpose Herb Blend or thyme, basil, salt, cheese, and cayenne pepper. Mix well. Cut baguette in half lengthwise. Generously spread each half with the butter mixture and garnish with paprika. Place under broiler uncovered until golden brown. Delectable!

TORTILLA EGG SCRAMBLE

1 duck egg
2 organic corn tortillas cut into bite-size pieces
1 tablespoon organic, unsalted butter
¼ cup red onion, chopped
½ cup Roma tomato, chopped
1 teaspoon elephant garlic, grated
2 tablespoons FCP extra virgin olive oil
1 tablespoon lemon juice (optional)
¼ teaspoon RealSalt
Cayenne pepper to taste

Place half of the chopped tomato in a bowl with the garlic, oil, lemon juice, salt, and pepper; stir and set aside. Preheat a medium skillet and melt butter. Add onion and sauté until lightly browned. Stir in tortilla pieces and cook for 2 minutes. Whisk in egg and cook until done, stirring to scramble. Spoon salsa over and serve immediately. Delicioso!

TROPICAL SMOOTHIE

    1 cup fresh or frozen papaya chunks
    1 cup fresh or frozen pineapple chunks
    1 pear, cut and peeled
    ½ cup goat's milk
    ½ cup coconut milk or coconut sorbet
    ¼ cup Grade B maple syrup or 1 tablespoon raw honey
    2 tablespoons goat's yogurt
    1 teaspoon lecithin powder (non-GMO)
    4-6 ice cubes

Peel papaya, pineapple, and pear. Cut into bite-size pieces and place in blender. Pour in goat's milk, coconut milk, yogurt, ice cubes, and maple syrup. Blend on high until smooth. Pour into 8-ounce glasses and serve. Refrigerate any unused portion immediately to preserve freshness, enzymes, and live cultures. Try it as a sauce over fresh fruit.

TROPICAL TRAIL MIX

    1 cup raw almonds
    1 cup raw cashews
    1 cup dried pineapple, cut bite size
    ½ cup coconut, shredded, unsweetened
    ½ cup dried papaya and or mango, unsweetened

Combine all ingredients in a glass bowl and mix well. Keep refrigerated with a tight-fitting lid. Great for snacks on the run!

TROUT WITH HERBED BUTTER

4 fillets rainbow trout, wild-caught
¼ cup Herbed Butter (*see recipe on page 173*)
1 teaspoon elephant garlic, pressed
1 lemon, cut into wedges
¼ cup fresh lemon juice
1 tablespoon safflower oil
1 tablespoon lecithin powder (non-GMO)
1 teaspoon paprika
1 teaspoon capers

Rinse and pat dry fillets. Place in a glass baking dish coated in safflower oil; spread the butter on each fillet. Broil for 10 minutes or until browned and flakey. Trout should be brown and flaky. In a saucepan, heat oil. Combine capers, lemon juice, paprika, and salt and pepper to taste. Whisk in lecithin powder to thicken. Pour sauce over trout, garnish with lemon wedges, and serve immediately.

UDON N'CHEESE

1 8.8-ounce package Udon noodles
1 cup goat's Gouda cheese, grated
1 teaspoon Bragg Liquid Aminos
1 cup broccoli florets, coarsely chopped
1 tablespoon organic unsalted butter
½ cup organic heavy cream
1 tablespoon Pecorino Romano cheese, grated
½ teaspoon cayenne pepper
½ teaspoon RealSalt

In large stainless-steel pot, boil 6 cups fresh water. Add Udon noodles and simmer for 6 minutes or until done. Do not overcook. Drain noodles. Add butter, Gouda cheese, cream, yeast flakes, and liquid aminos; toss over low flame until cheese is melted. Add raw broccoli, RealSalt, and cayenne pepper. Arrange noodles in a serving dish and garnish with Pecorino Romano cheese.

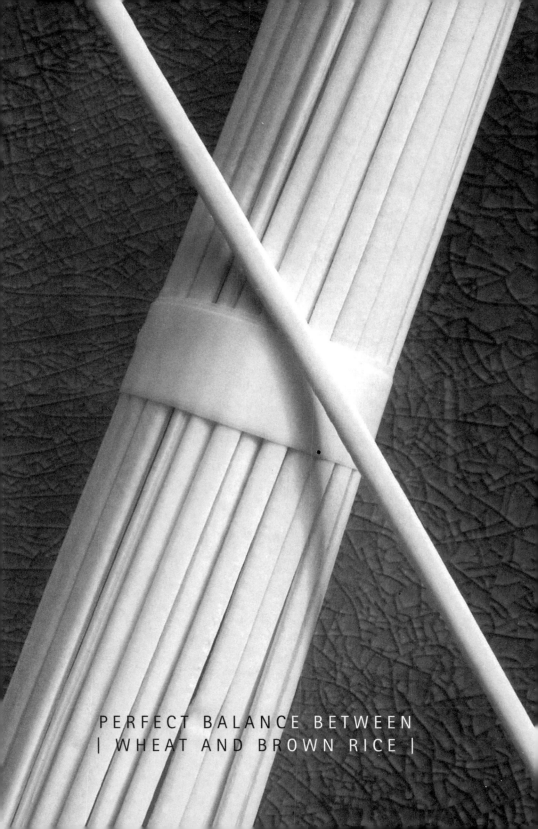

PERFECT BALANCE BETWEEN
| WHEAT AND BROWN RICE |

UDON TOSSED WITH ASPARAGUS AND ELEPHANT GARLIC

1 pound asparagus

1 8.8-ounce package Udon noodles

¼ cup natural spring water

3 tablespoons organic unsalted butter

RealSalt and cayenne pepper to taste

1 tablespoon elephant garlic, freshly grated
   or 1 teaspoon elephant garlic blend

1 teaspoon lecithin powder

Wash asparagus spears well and place them in a bowl of filtered water with 1 drop food-grade hydrogen peroxide. Drain and place asparagus on paper towels. Cut asparagus in thirds on the diagonal. Keep refrigerated until ready to use.

Pour water into a large stainless-steel pot. Bring to a boil, add Udon noodles, and simmer for 7 to 10 minutes, being careful not to overcook. Carefully drain into a large colander in the sink. Place butter and cut asparagus into pot; pour hot noodles over asparagus. Toss with elephant garlic, salt, cayenne, and lecithin powder. Garnish with lemon wedges.

THE ULTIMATE QUICHE

3 duck eggs

1 cup goat's Gouda cheese, grated

1 cup organic heavy cream

1 cup red potato, grated

½ cup leek, thinly sliced

¼ cup red onion, chopped

3 tablespoons Pecorino Romano cheese, grated

1 teaspoon dried thyme

1 teaspoon dried oregano

1 teaspoon RealSalt

Dash cayenne pepper

½ cup artichoke hearts, sliced

Garnish with fresh sprig of thyme and paprika

Preheat oven to 375 degrees. In a large mixing bowl combine cheeses, vegetables, herbs, and spices; toss well. In a separate bowl, whisk eggs, cream, and salt. Combine the two mixtures, whisking thoroughly; pour into piecrust-lined quiche dish.

Bake for 1 hour or until top is golden brown and center is firm.

VANILLA YOGURT

1 cup goat's yogurt
1 tablespoon Grade B maple syrup
½ teaspoon vanilla extract, alcohol-free

Mix all ingredients in a glass bowl for one serving. Chill.

WILD ARUGULA SALAD

12 ounces wild arugula
1 small avocado
½ cup sprouted wheat berries
¼ cup dried currants

Rinse arugula thoroughly in fresh water with 1 drop food-grade hydrogen peroxide. Place in salad spinner to drain. Combine with avocado and sprouted wheat berries. Toss with Simple Dressing (*see recipe on page 196*).

WILD LOX AND BAGEL

2 halves sprouted wheat bagel,
   lightly toasted
4 to 8 slices smoked wild Alaskan salmon
4 ounces soft goat's cheese
1 Roma tomato, halved and sliced
½ red onion, thinly sliced
2 pickles, sliced
1 large avocado, sliced
2 teaspoons organic capers
1 tablespoon FCP extra virgin olive oil
Dash RealSalt

On a serving platter, arrange individual sections of tomato, onion, pickles, and avocado. Add capers to the middle. Pour olive oil on avocado and sprinkle with a dash of salt. Refrigerate until ready to use.

Cut each bagel in half. Lightly toast and place on a plate. Spread each bagel half with 1 ounce of goat's cheese and layer salmon evenly on each one. I like Alvarado St. Bakery bagels.

YAM CHIPS

2 medium garnet yams,
  peeled and sliced ⅛-inch thick
½ cup safflower oil
1 tablespoon organic unsalted butter
1 tablespoon Grade B maple syrup
½ teaspoon dried thyme
RealSalt to taste

In a large skillet, heat oil. Line the bottom with yam slices and cook over medium flame for 1 minute per side or until lightly browned. Drain on a paper towel. Repeat until all chips are done. Arrange on a platter and drizzle with maple syrup sauce. For sauce, melt butter in a small saucepan; add maple syrup, thyme, and salt and stir until heated and serve.

If you prefer, maple sauce can be served on the side for dipping. Serves 2 to 4.

For Raw Yam Chips

Simply wash, peel, cut yam into desired shape and enjoy!

YOGURT AND CUCUMBER

2 cups goat's yogurt
2 medium Persian cucumbers, peeled and chopped
1 teaspoon dried mint
1 teaspoon lecithin powder (non-GMO)
½ teaspoon RealSalt
Dash cayenne pepper

Gently combine all ingredients in a glass storage bowl. Cover tightly and refrigerate. For best results use mixture within 24 hours. Serves 4.

YOGURT WITH FRESH BERRIES

1 cup goat's yogurt, plain
½ cup fresh berries
1 teaspoon raw honey or 1 tablespoon Grade B maple syrup

In a bowl combine yogurt and honey or syrup. Stir until blended. Fold in berries. Keep refrigerated until ready to eat. If you are hurried, blend with two to three ice cubes and take it to go! This is a great way to help balance flora and fauna (good bacteria) in the small intestine.

YOGURT WITH FRESH CROOKNECK SQUASH

1 whole crookneck squash, shredded
2 cups goat's yogurt
1 teaspoon dried dill
½ teaspoon RealSalt
Dash cayenne pepper

Combine all ingredients in a glass mixing bowl and mix well. Keep chilled until ready to serve. Great side dish and sauce for fish too!

YOGURT WITH SAUTÉED CROOKNECK SQUASH

3 whole crookneck squash, sliced
2 cups goat's yogurt
¼ cup safflower oil
1 teaspoon dried dill
½ teaspoon RealSalt
½ teaspoon turmeric
Dash cayenne pepper

In medium skillet heat oil, add a dash of turmeric into the pan, add squash slices, lightly brown on each side. Using a pair of long cooking tongs, turn slices and drain on a paper towel lined plate; set aside until ready to use. Continue this process until all slices are cooked. In a mixing bowl combine yogurt, salt, dill, and cayenne; stir well. In a large glass serving dish, layer yogurt and squash slices, alternating until all slices are used. A tasty and festive way to serve yogurt, this recipe can be served as an appetizer or side dish.

ZESTY CATCH-UP

3 ounces sun-dried Roma tomatoes, hydrated

1 cup boiled natural spring water

1 teaspoon elephant garlic, pressed

½ teaspoon garlic powder

¼ cup raw honey
  or ¼ cup grade B maple syrup

¼ teaspoon ground cinnamon

¼ teaspoon ground cloves

½ teaspoon paprika

¼ cup red wine vinegar

¼ teaspoon RealSalt

Dash cayenne pepper

In a glass mixing bowl combine tomatoes and garlic; pour in boiled water and cover 15 minutes or until tomatoes are hydrated. Pour mixture into blender, cover, and blend until smooth. Combine with remaining ingredients, blend until smooth. Place in glass jar with tight-fitting lid. Keep refrigerated until ready to use.

Appendix A

Vitamins

Vitamin A

Prevents night blindness and other eye problems as well as skin disorders like acne

Good food sources: apricots, asparagus, beet greens, broccoli, cantaloupe, dandelion greens, dulse, garlic, kale, mustard greens, papayas, peaches, spinach, spirulina, Swiss chard, watercress

Good herb sources: alfalfa, cayenne, fennel seed, hops, horsetail, kelp, lemongrass, nettles, paprika, peppermint, raspberry leaf, red clover, sage, watercress

Vitamin B1 (thiamine)

Enhances circulation and assists in blood formation, carbohydrate metabolism and the production of hydrochloric acid essential for proper digestion

Good food sources: almonds, asparagus, barley, brewer's yeast, broccoli, brown rice, cashews, egg yolks (duck), raisins (red), sunflower seeds, whole wheat, wheat germ

Good herb sources: alfalfa, cayenne, chamomile, fennel seed, fenugreek, hops, nettle, peppermint, raspberry leaf, red clover, sage

Vitamin B2 (riboflavin)

Necessary for red blood cell formation, antibody production, cell respiration and growth

Good food sources: almonds, asparagus, avocado, barley, broccoli, brewer's yeast, cashews, goat's milk and cheese, kale, mushrooms, sunflower seeds

Good herb sources: alfalfa, cayenne, chamomile, fennel seed, fenugreek, American ginseng, hops, horsetail, nettle, peppermint, raspberry leaves, red clover, sage

Vitamin B3 (niacin, nicotinic acid, niacinamide)

Needed for proper circulation and healthy skin

Good food sources: almonds, asparagus, avocado, barley, brewer's yeast, broccoli, cashews, corn meal, dates, goat's milk and cheese, mushrooms, red potato, sunflower seeds, wheat germ, organic whole wheat products

Vitamin B5 (pantothenic acid)

Needed for production of adrenal hormones, helps the body utilize vitamins, and improves stamina

Good food sources: brewer's yeast, duck eggs, red kidney beans, royal jelly, sesame seeds, sunflower seeds

Vitamin B6 (pyridoxine)

Necessary for physical and mental health, brain function, immunity

Good food sources: almonds, brewer's yeast, brown rice, soybeans, honey, sunflower seeds, wheat germ

Vitamin B12 (cyanocobalamin)

Needed to prevent anemia and nerve damage, essential for cell division, promotes normal growth and development, helps regulate red blood cells and utilization of iron

Excellent food sources: bison, duck eggs, and whole wheat

Good food sources: dulse, kelp, goat cheese, brewer's yeast, organic soy products, wheat germ

Good herb sources: alfalfa, hops

> Adequate consumption of **FRESH**
> fruit and **VEGETABLES** provides
> **BRAIN FOOD** and energy in the
> form of folic acid

Did you know that your body cannot use B vitamins without potassium?

The above information on B vitamins is provided as a guide to their super food sources. For the body to benefit from any single B vitamin it must be taken together with the whole spectrum of B vitamins (B1 through B12). Furthermore, no B vitamins can be utilized without potassium, so any B-complex supplement must be accompanied by potassium supplementation. If no potassium is present, the B vitamins will simply pass as waste through your urine.

(So remember to take B-complex supplements from a food source combined with potassium!)

Biotin

Helps metabolize carbohydrates, fats, and proteins with the utilization of B vitamins

Good food sources: brown rice, brewer's yeast, cashews, duck eggs, goat's milk, wild-caught orange roughy

Choline

Needed for proper transmission of nerve impulses from the brain through the central nervous system; also needed to regulate the gallbladder, liver function, and lecithin formation

Good food sources: duck eggs, non-GMO lecithin, soybeans

Folic Acid (folate)

Brain food needed for energy production, formation of red blood cells, and necessary for any cell replication

Good food sources: asparagus, arugula, butter lettuce, fresh dates, endive, fresh mushrooms (like crimini, shitake, chanterelle), kale, spinach, raw red potatoes, Swiss chard

Inositol

Vital for hair growth, helps reduce cholesterol levels, helps prevent hardening of the arteries, and helps remove fat from the liver; necessary for the formation of lecithin to metabolize fat and cholesterol

Good food sources: brown rice, brewer's yeast, cantaloupe, cashews, citrus fruits (tangerines, mandarin oranges, lemons and limes) soybeans, wheat germ

PABA (para amino benzoic acid)

Member of the B vitamins and part of the folic acid molecule; aids in the metabolism and utilization of amino acids and supports red blood cells

Good food sources: brewer's yeast, wheat germ, whole grains such as brown rice, duck eggs, blackstrap molasses

Vitamin C (ascorbic acid)

An antioxidant: it boosts the immune system and helps lower LDL and increase HDL, which can help to prevent atherosclerosis. Because our body does not produce ascorbic acid, we must supplement daily to receive its many other important benefits.

Good food sources: avocado, asparagus, red beet, raspberries, strawberries, blackberries, kiwi, lemon, tangerine, lime, star fruit, honeydew, cantaloupe, papaya, kale, broccoli, cauliflower, Roma and Heirloom tomatoes, asparagus, mustard greens, red potato, pineapple, mango, pineapple, Swiss chard, watercress

Good herb sources: alfalfa, cayenne, fennel seed, fenugreek, hops, horsetail, kelp, peppermint, nettle, paprika, red raspberry leaf, red clover

Bioflavonoids

Essential for the absorption of vitamin C; used in the treatment of athletic injuries because they relieve pain, bumps, and bruises

Good food sources: the white material just beneath citrus fruits like tangerines, lemons, and limes, apricot, blackberries, cherries, dark grapes, Roma or Heirloom tomato, papaya, cantaloupe, plums, prunes

Good herb sources: hawthorn berry, horsetail

Vitamin D

Most important immune vitamin, a fat-soluble vitamin required for the absorption and utilization of calcium and phosphorus; necessary for normal growth of bones and teeth in children, protects against muscle weakness, and helps regulate heartbeat

Good food sources: duck eggs, goat's milk, goat butter, and wild-caught salmon. Please note that vitamin D from a food source is second best, and regular exposure to the sun is the only way to get vitamin D, which is the most active and is considered the natural form of vitamin D

The best natural source: wholesome sunlight. Sun exposure for 20 minutes a day is an effective way to absorb vitamin D because it allows your body to synthesize vitamin D in the skin from the sun's ultraviolet rays.

Vitamin E

An antioxidant that is important in the prevention of cancer and cardiovascular disease: improves circulation and is necessary for tissue repair. It prevents cell damage by inhibiting the oxidation of lipids (fats) and the formation of free radicals.

Good food sources: figs, asparagus, broccoli, brown rice, whole wheat, first cold pressed oils like olive oil, wheat germ oil, and safflower oil

Vitamin K

Essential for bone repair and blood clotting, it promotes healthy liver function and may increase resistance to infection in children.

Good food sources: arugula, asparagus, broccoli, butter lettuce, cauliflower, kale, spinach, safflower oil, Swiss chard, goat's yogurt. Also synthesized by bacteria in the intestines

Appendix B

Macro-Minerals

Organic Calcium

Maintains muscle and digestive system health, builds bone, neutralizes acidity, and clears toxins: helps prevent muscle cramps, maintains regular heartbeat, and helps in the transmission of nerve impulses

> **Good food sources:** goat's and sheep's milk, cheese, and yogurt, sesame seeds, broccoli, figs, almonds, spinach, kale, and watercress

Magnesium

Causes strong peristalsis, builds bone, increases flexibility, and increases alkalinity: helps metabolize minerals and carbohydrates and protects arterial linings from stress caused by sudden blood pressure changes

> **Good food sources:** almonds, avocados, bananas, cantaloupe, cashews, whole wheat, soy, barley, brown rice, corn, figs, apricots, blackstrap molasses, lemons, Swiss chard, broccoli, spinach, organic tofu, kale, arugula, asparagus, wild-caught salmon, kelp

> **Good herb sources:** alfalfa, cayenne, chamomile, hops, horsetail, fennel seed, fenugreek, lemongrass, nettle, paprika, peppermint, raspberry leaf, red clover, sage

Phosphorous

Required component of bones and energy processing. It is needed for blood clotting, cell growth, heart and kidney functions.

Good food sources: asparagus, brewer's yeast, wild-caught salmon, sesame and sunflower seeds

Potassium

Required electrolyte needed to maintain pH in the bloodstream. It helps maintain a healthy nervous system and regular heart rhythm; it also functions in stroke prevention.

Good food sources: figs, almonds, apricot, avocado, sun-ripened bananas, lima beans, blackstrap molasses, kiwi, broccoli, cashews, Swiss chard, spinach, yams, dates, endives, guava, horseradish, mushrooms, peach, plum, red potato, Roma tomato, whole wheat, whole barley, brewer's yeast

Good herb sources: hops, horsetail, nettle, red clover, sage

Organic Sodium

Electrolyte necessary for maintaining proper water balance and blood pH; also needed for stomach, nerve, and muscle function

Good food sources: Though virtually all foods contain some sodium, one of the best food sources is RealSalt brand sea salt from Redmond, Utah.

Sulfur

Needed for the synthesis of collagen, disinfects the blood and helps the body resist bacteria. Due to its ability to protect against the harmful effects of radiation and pollution, it slows the aging process.

Good food sources: red kidney beans, elephant garlic, kale, soybeans, wheat germ

Good herb sources: horsetail or shave grass. The amino acids cystine, lysine, and methionine also contain sulfur.

Trace Minerals

Cobalt

Required for biosynthesis of vitamin B12 family of coenzymes

Good food sources: goat and sheep cheese and dairy, bison meat, and seaweed

Copper

Needed for healthy nerves and joints: essential for the formation of collagen, and works in balance with zinc and vitamin C to form elastin for healthy skin; involved in the healing process and energy production

Good food sources: almonds; avocados; barley; red kidney beans; white beans; red beets; blackstrap molasses; broccoli; crimini; shitake and chanterelle mushrooms; kale; spinach; wild-caught salmon

Iodine

Helps to maintain a healthy thyroid gland and metabolize excess fat; important for physical and mental development; helps to prevent goiter

Good food sources: kelp, seaweed, agar-agar, asparagus, dulse, elephant garlic, lima beans, sesame seeds, soybeans, spinach, Swiss chard. Redmond brand RealSalt provides nature's own balance of minerals.

Iron

Required for a healthy immune system and for energy production; needed to produce hemoglobin and myoglobin and for the oxygenation of red blood cells

Good food sources: almonds, avocados, bison, red beets, blackstrap molasses, brewer's yeast, blackberries, cherries, Concord grapes, dates, dulse, duck eggs, kale, kelp, kidney and lima beans, red lentils, millet, dried prunes, red raisins, brown rice, sesame seeds, soybeans, Swiss chard, watercress, wild-caught salmon, and aged red wine

Good herb sources: alfalfa, cayenne, chamomile, dandelion, fennel seed, fenugreek, horsetail, kelp, lemongrass, nettles, paprika, peppermint, raspberry leaf, and sarsaparilla

Manganese

Needed for protein and fat metabolism, healthy nerves and ducts, a healthy immune system, and blood sugar regulation

Good food sources: avocado, pineapple, kale, spinach

Good herb sources: alfalfa, chamomile, dandelion, fennel seed, fenugreek, American ginseng, hops, horsetail, lemongrass, peppermint, red raspberry leaf, red clover, and wild yam

Selenium

Functions as an antioxidant in partnership with vitamin E to maintain a healthy heart and liver; regulates the effects of thyroid hormone on fat metabolism

Good food sources: Brazil nuts, brewer's yeast, broccoli, brown rice, kelp, red onion, wild-caught salmon, whole wheat

Good herb sources: alfalfa, cayenne, chamomile, fennel seed, fenugreek, elephant garlic, American ginseng, hawthorn berry, hops, horsetail, lemongrass, nettle, peppermint, red raspberry leaf, sarsaparilla

Zinc

The most important mineral for skin; essential for prostate/uterine gland functions and growth of the reproductive organs; may help prevent acne and regulate the activity of oil glands; promotes a healthy immune system and the healing of wounds; protects the liver from chemical damage and is vital for bone formation

Good food sources: avocado, asparagus, barley, legumes, lima beans, sunflower seeds, whole wheat

Good herb sources: alfalfa, cayenne, chamomile, dandelion, fennel seed, hops, nettle, sage, sarsaparilla, wild yam

Electrolytes

Substances that dissolve in water to form solutions that can conduct an electrical current. The balance of the electrolytes in our bodies is essential for normal function of our cells and our organs. Some important electrolytes include organic sodium, which is the major positive ion in the fluid outside of cells, and potassium anion found inside of cells. Chloride is the major anion (negatively charged ion) found in the fluid outside of cells and in blood. RealSalt solution has almost the same concentration of chloride ion as human fluids.

Chlorophyll

The green pigment of plant leaves and algae is vital for photosynthesis and allows plants to obtain energy from sunlight. One of the strongest anti-oxidants in nature, chlorophyll strengthens our cells, making us less susceptible to harmful bacteria. It is excellent for neutralizing toxins and boosting immunity. Some good food sources are alfalfa sprouts, barley grass, kale, and wheatgrass.

Appendix C

21-Day Colon Cleanse

The First Phase

The first phase (5-7 days) is gentle and starts with at least two alkalizing meals daily—no meats, but plenty of raw salad and low sugar/high enzyme fruits such as papaya, raspberries, strawberries, and blackberries. Smoothies can be made with fresh tangerine juice (not pasteurized) and goat's yogurt. Take 1 teaspoon fennel seed in a vegetarian gel capsule to soften mucous plaque. During this 21-day period it is imperative to drink at least 8 glasses of water per day.

The most important part of this cleanse is the *daily blended drink* consisting of 32 ounces of freshly made organic vegetables, consumed throughout the day, with the following ingredients:

> 2 to 3 medium Roma tomatoes, chopped
> ½ medium red beet, peeled and chopped
> ¼ bunch cilantro, chopped
> 2 to 3 inches of a stalk of leek, chopped
> 1 whole lemon, juiced
> 1 tablespoon fresh ginger, peeled and sliced
> ⅓ whole cucumber, peeled and chopped
> 6-8 ounces of arrowhead water
> ½ teaspoon RealSalt

Continue on this phase until cleansing reactions such as aches, general weakness, chills, diarrhea, and gas dissipate. You will have a feeling of euphoria, increased energy, restful sleep, and clearer thinking. Once equilibrium is established and light-headedness is diminished, you can proceed to the second phase.

If a salad is missed, don't worry. The cleansing benefits are maintained by the vegetable drink.

The Second Phase

The second phase (7 days) is intermediate and requires continuation of phase one. However, alkalizing meals are reduced to one daily. Increase water intake and fresh juices as needed to maintain energy and vitality. Next add the following herbs: alfalfa, kelp, horsetail, hawthorne berry, and marshmallow. Also include a variety of the following in your juice and water: psyllium husk, alfalfa seeds, flax seeds, and/or millet. For ease and efficiency psyllium may be taken in capsules. Bentonite clay powder in capsules will expedite this phase and enhance the overall cleansing process. During this phase lactobacillus, acidophilus, and bifidobacterium bifidum supplements help to maintain the friendly bacteria in the colon. As the amount of solid food intake decreases, digestion is relieved from its normal tasks and can devote energy to cleansing priorities. Stay on this phase until bowel movements have stabilized.

Remember: the daily vegetable drink is an essential for maximizing the effects of this cleanse—you must have it consistently.

The Third Phase

The third and final phase is very powerful and requires determination to follow through. No meals. This includes fruits (dried raisin/cranberries), raw red potatoes, or avocados. Only consume herbs and water and increase quantities of the daily vegetable drink. Chlorophyll or INS wheatgrass drinks may be added to the final phase, which is a maximum of one week.

During this phase you may experience the following:

Mucous plaque will be expelled in small chunks or can be in sections up to several feet long. When we stop eating (as long as nutrients are present), our bodies begin to seek out stored and putrefied proteins and fats that are killing our cells. Imagine removing excesses that are clogging, blocking, and destroying tissues, organs, and entire systems of the body. You will experience a thorough physical cleansing and also heightened mental clarity, emotional balance, and enhanced sensory perception.

I encourage you to stay on track once you have embarked on this intense cleansing journey. The reward is worth it!

Cleansing Salad

6 ounces Baby Spring mix or butter lettuce
avocado
Roma tomatoes
red onion
broccoli
alfalfa sprouts

Dressing

extra virgin olive oil
lemon juice (not vinegar)
dried or fresh thyme, basil, oregano, and marjoram
RealSalt and cayenne pepper to taste

Raw almonds, cashews and sunflower seeds with dried cranberries and raisins are allowed.

Raw red potato peeled and sliced with RealSalt, mashed avocado, and olive oil are also allowed during the first phase and enhance the cleansing process.

Vegetables for variety

cauliflower, crookneck squash, asparagus, raw pine nuts, arugula, green beans, and chives

Avoid

coffee
red kidney beans
dairy products (except for goat's yogurt)
all sweeteners: sucanat, honey, maple syrup or brown rice syrup.

Herb and seed regimen, phase one

1 teaspoon flaxseeds daily

Twice daily
alfalfa seeds
fennel seeds
1 level teaspoon bentonite clay
   or 3 capsules morning and night

Twice daily
3 capsules psyllium husk (for the first time)
4 capsules or 1 teaspoon extract golden seal root
4 capsules or 1 teaspoon extract red raspberry leaves
4 capsules or 1 teaspoon extract myrrh gum
4 capsules or 1 teaspoon extract peppermint

Phase two additions
4 capsules or 1 teaspoon extract kelp
4 capsules or 1 teaspoon extract horsetail
4 capsules or 1 teaspoon extract hawthorn berry
4 capsules or 1 teaspoon extract marshmallow
3 capsules twice daily acidophilus/bifidus (must be refrigerated)
   or ¾ teaspoon powdered pro-biotic microbes

Phase three additions
1 ounce wheatgrass juice or 1 sachet INS wheatgrass powder
1 teaspoon liquid chlorophyll with water
Tea is allowed but made only from the above-mentioned herbs.

The colon cleanse once every year will promote health and rejuvenation throughout the body. After the first time it could take only 4 to 5 days for each phase, reducing the cleansing period 12 to 15 days total.

Gradual reintroduction of food is essential after completion of this cleanse. The first day fresh fruits and fruit juices are best. The second day, soup and salad with raw nuts (remember to chew thoroughly) is allowed. By the third day, smaller portions of regular meals are fine.

Warning: *This cleanse may be suitable only for individuals with optimum liver function. Please consult your health care practitioner.*

Index

C

D

M

N

O

Osekihan, 177
over-eating, effects of, 34

P

PABA (para amino benzoic acid), 220
Pan-Broiled Wasabi Salmon, 178
pancreas, role in digestion of, 12, 13, 14, 25–26
pantothenic acid, 218
Papaya Smoothie, 178
Papua New Guinea Coffee, 28, 93, 180
peanut butter, 27
Pears with Chocolate Sauce, 180–181
pH balance, enzymes and, 13–14, 23–24
phosphorus, 224
Pineapple Soda, 181
Pineapple Upside-Down Cake, 181–182
Pineapple with Honey Yogurt Sauce, 182
Pink Pear Pie, 182–183
Pita Pocket Sandwich, 183
Plance, Donald, 86
plants (in household), 85–86
Pommes a La Christara, 184
pork products, 48
potassium, 224
potato water extract, 25
poultry, 48
produce, washing, 7
proteins
    complete combinations, 79
    function of, 31

sources of, 31, 41
pyridoxine, 218

Q

Quick Fries, 185
Quick Sandwich Spread, 185
Quick Strawberry Sorbet, 185
Quick-Fried Beans, 184

R

Raphaology, alcohol use in, 67
Raw Almond Milk, 186
raw foods, 10, 14, 34–36, 77, 78, 90
Raw Soaked Almonds, 186
RealSalt, 54–55
Red Bean Burrito, 186–187
Red Enchiladas, 187
Red Lentil Soup, 188
Red Potato Flower Salad, 189
Red Potato Leek Soup, 189
Red Rice with Bison, 190–191
red wine, 65
riboflavin, 217–218
Rubin, Jordan S.

S

sake, 66
salad dressings
    Avocado Dressing, 131
    Creamy Lemon Dressing, 156
    for Arugula, Avocado, and Fennel Salad, 129
    Honey Mustard Dressing, 174

living beyond organic

PHOTOS ©iStockphoto.com: front cover, pear, portishead1; front cover, persimmons, Yuri_Arcurs; front cover and throughout interior, abstract green swash, oblachko; front flap, spice list and utensils, DNY59; page xiv, kale, MentalArt; xx, pills, damircudic; 68, yams, YinYang; 80, elephant garlic in skillet, carterphoto; 96, coffee and English muffins, Juanmonino; 125, almonds, GeoffBlack; 126, muffins, buck5150; 129, olive oil, YasmineV; 132, spinach salad, creacart; 135, sorbet, ShyMan; 136, mixed berries, ilmwa555; 139, cayenne pepper, Geminai; 140, Roma tomatoes, gimletup; 149, olives on branch, paolozawa; 150, fennel, egal; 158, eggs in bowl, FotografiaBasica; 161, cucumber slices, groveb; 169, shrimp kabobs, THEPALMER; 171, avocados, eyewave; 172, thyme, eyewave; 174, salmon fillet, og-vision; 176, cookies, sbonk; 179, marble countertop, sbayram; 188, lentils, timsa; 194, basmati rice cup, R0b; 199, mangoes, absolutely_frenchy; 204, dill, Tomboy2290; 207, dried pineapple, WinterWitch; 209, Udon noodles, ACMPhoto; 211, arugula, ProPhotos; 212, bagels with wheat, coldblade.

PHOTOS from BigStockPhoto.com: page 4, papaya and avocado, ©joanE; 179, raw salmon, ©Belle Momenti; 215, yogurt, ©looby

PHOTOS ©Can Stock Photo Inc.: page 167, garlic, DLeonis; 192, sesame seeds, Riverlim; 203, pancakes, robynmac

PHOTOS ©Ulead Systems: endsheets, avocado; page 76, asparagus